How to be a   ....

...and other handy stuff for working with people

Matt Shiells-Jones

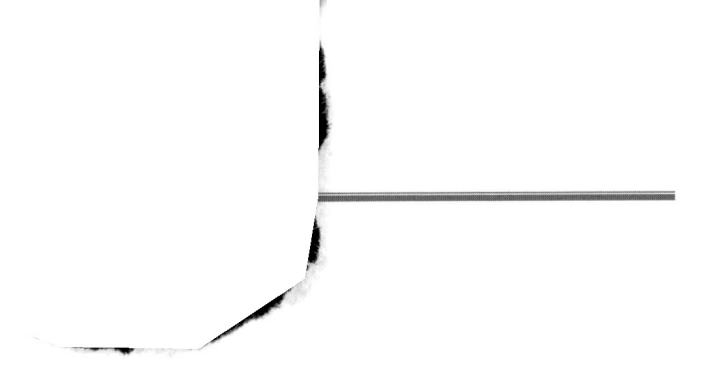

To David,

Because you let me live my dream!

Copyright © 2012 Matthew Shiells-Jones

All Rights Reserved
ISBN: 978-1-4716-0699-1

ALL RIGHTS RESERVED. This book contains material protected under International and Federal Copyright Laws and Treaties. Any unauthorized reprint or use of this material is prohibited. No part of this book may be reproduced or transmitted in any form or by any means, electronic or mechanical, including photocopying, recording, or by any information storage and retrieval system without express written permission from the author / publisher.

About the Author

Matt Shiells-Jones was born in Dorset in 1981. His hospitality career began when he was just 13 in Torquay, Devon where he became employed as a restaurant waiter and porter.

He quickly learnt to love the hospitality industry and spent many years working in restaurants and as a general assistant before moving to Sheffield. It was here that Matt worked in contact centres fielding sales and customer service calls. This allowed him to become a receptionist when he moved to Blackpool due to missing the hotel industry.

He quickly progressed into Front of House Management and soon became a specialist in his field, dealing with complaints and over bookings without batting an eyelid. He spent time training new receptionists for several hotels and even spent several years training contact centre advisors in complaint handling and customer management.

He now resides in Manchester, where he continues to work in Hospitality Management, building on his nearly 20 years of experience.

Follow Matt on Twitter: **MShiells_Jones**

Foreword

This book started life as a training manual but quickly grew into something far beyond a basic step by step guide. Once I started writing, everything just kept flowing and I found it hard to stop.

I have covered a variety of different subjects within this book and hope to continue adding more as time goes on – this is only the beginning! I think I have covered as much as I can about reception and front of house and I hope people get a lot out of this. It is designed to be a fairly easy read (although there are some intense sections), but I wanted to ensure that everyone who reads this understands the complexities of a receptionist role and has the background knowledge to help them through those tougher moments. I wrote this to take into account everyone from management level to ground level and I hope that everyone throughout these levels will take some important lessons on guest service from this book!

If you like the book, please review it as such; if you think I missed something out, please let me know; if you did not like the book, it was written by some other guy!

Oh, one final thing – if this book asks you a question, please think about the answer to it! Do not just carry on reading, take a second to read it and think about it! This is just so you get the most out of this book!

Matt

Contents

About the Author 3
Foreword 4
Contents 5
"I am a Front Desk Agent" 11
Before we begin 14
Your Role 15
Interpersonal Skills 18
    Colleagues 18
    Guests 21
        1.   Each guest is unique 21
        2.   Every guest has the right to have high expectations of you 23
        3.   Every guest has the right to complain 24
        4.   Each guest is your boss 24
    Organisation 25
    My Reception Desk: 27
Negotiation 28
Stages of negotiation 32
    Stage 1 32
    Stage 2 33
    Stage 3 34
    When negotiation fails 36
Call handling 37
    Greeting the Call 38
        Rule 1 – Do not make it too informal 39
        Rule 2 – Always state your name and that of your hotel 40
        Rule 3 – Always be prepared for the call 40
    So, to the middle… 40
        Blind Transfer 41
        Introduced Transfers 43

Contents

Reservation Enquiries 44
Ending the call 46
    For reservations 46
    For general enquiries 46
Sales Skills 47
I.T Skills 50
Multitasking 52
The Guest Journey 54
    Driving the decision 54
    Email Bookings 56
    Pre-arrival Checks 58
- Rates 58
- Deposits 58
- Guest information 59
- Room information 59
- Additional Requests 59
- Pass on Information 59

    Routing 60
    Allocating rooms 61
    Allocation Crossover 63
    How do you allocate rooms effectively? 66
    1. Room location 67
    2. Room type booked 68
    3. Additional beds or cots 68
    4. VIP status 68
    5. Booking requests 68
    6. Everything else 68

Arrival Day 70
    Printing registration cards 70
    Group Check-In 73
    Single Check-in 75

Contents

- Post Check-In 79
- Hotel with no life 81
- Engaging the guest 83
  - Wedding Guests: 83
  - Leisure guests: 83
  - Business Guests: 83
  - Airport Guests: 83
  - Guidelines 85
  - Dealing with offensive remarks 86
- Complaint Handling 89
  - Complainer Types 89
    - Silent Complainer 89
    - Social Complainer 90
    - Empathetic Complainers 91
    - Assertive Complainers 91
    - Aggressive Complainer 92
    - Professional Complainer 93
    - Compensatory Complainer 93
  - The Three C's 96
    - Confident 96
    - Calm 97
    - Collected 97
  - Common Complaints 98
  - Wants versus Needs 99
  - The Complaint Triangle 102
    - Cause 102
    - Emotion 105
    - Desire 106
  - Standardisation 109
  - Transference 111
  - Handling that complaint 112

How to be a Hotel Receptionist...   Page 7

Contents

- Email/Written Complaints 112
    - Assessing the complaint 114
    - Determining a response 115
    - Sample Response 119
- Face to face complaints 121
- DEAL with it 122
    - Divert 122
    - Empathise 122
    - Ask 122
    - Listen 122
- The magic question 123
- Responding face to face 125
    - Repeat 125
    - State your position 125
    - Gain understanding 125
    - Follow up 125
- Points to take on board with complaint resolution offers 127
- Overbookings 129
    - Causes of overbooking 131
        - High demand for your hotel 131
        - High demand in the local area 131
    - How to out-book 132
        - General out-booking. 132
        - Proactive Out-Booking 132
        - Reactive Out-Booking 133
    - General Guidelines 134
- Cash handling 136
- Shift Checklists 138
- Keys 140
    - Lock-outs 141
- Messages 142

Contents

Urgent or distressing messages 142
Non urgent messages 143
    Delivering messages 143
Events 144
    Any event: 144
    Conferences and Seminars: 144
    Weddings and Parties 145
Guest confidentiality 146
Marketing Materials 148
Departures 149
That's all folks... sort of 151
Emergency Measures: 152
  Guest arrives with booking confirmation from a travel agent, but no booking in your system: 152
  Guest screaming at you: 152
  Guest collapses: 153
  Armed Robbery 153
  Guest has been robbed/incident of theft 153
  Suspected food poisoning 154
  Guest leaves without paying 154
  A guest injures themselves 154
  A bedroom goes out of order 155
  A guest damages their room 155
  A guest smokes in their room 155
Glossary 156
Adapted Room 156
Allocation 156
Allocation Crossover 156
Arrival 156
Balancing Rooms 156
Check-in 157

Contents

Check-in 157

Close-out 157

Departure 158

ETA 158

Folio 158

Last-Let 158

Lock-out 158

No Show 158

Out booking 158

Out of Order 158

Out of Service 159

Overbooking 159

    Pre-Authorisation 159

Routing 159

"I am a Front Desk Agent"

> This poem was highlighted to me recently and I think it is a perfect addition to this book; I am unsure of who to attribute this to, or who wrote it or even when it first appeared, but it is fantastic and is 'oh so true'! If you wrote this, I hope you don't mind me using it; thank you for giving us our own statement of truth that is comical yet sadly true!

I have advanced degrees in Accounting, Public Relations, Marketing, Business, Computer Science, Civil Engineering, and Swahili. I can also read minds.

Of course I have the reservation that you booked six years ago even though you don't have the confirmation number and you think it was made under a name that starts with "S".

It is completely my fault that the blizzard shut down the airport and you have to sleep in a warm king-size bed while 5000 of your co-travellers are sleeping in benches at the airport. I am sorry.

It is not a problem for me to give you seven connecting, non-smoking, poolside suites with two king beds in each, four rollaways, 3 cribs, and yes, I can install a wet bar. I know it is my fault that we do not have a helicopter landing pad.

I am a Front Desk Agent. I am expected to speak all languages fluently. It is obvious to me that when you booked your reservation for Friday on the weekend we're sold out that you really meant Saturday. My company has entrusted me with all financial information and decisions, and yes, I am lying to you when I say we have no more rooms available. It is not a problem for

"I am a Front Desk Agent"

me to quickly construct several more guest rooms. THIS time I will not forget the helicopter landing pad. And it is my fault that everyone wanted to stay here. I should have known you were coming in, even though you had no reservation. After all, you stay at our brand of hotel all the time, 300 nights a year, and this is only the first time you've ever been to our city.

I am a front desk agent. I am quite capable of checking three people in, two people out, taking five reservations, answering fifteen incoming calls, delivering six bath towels to room 625, plunging the toilet in room 101, and restocking the supply of pool towels, all at the same time. Yes, I will be glad to call the van driver and tell him to drive over all the cars stuck in traffic because you've been waiting at the airport for 15 minutes and you've got jet lag.

I am a front desk agent, an operator, a bellhop, houseman, guest service representative, housekeeper, sales coordinator, information specialist, entertainment critic, restaurateur, stock broker, referee, janitor, computer technician, plumber, ice-breaker, postman, babysitter, dispatcher, laundry cleaner, lifeguard, electrician, ambassador, personal fitness trainer, fax expert, human jukebox, domestic abuse counsellor, and verbal punching bag. Yes, I know room 112 is not answering their phone. And of course I have their travel itinerary so I know exactly where they went when they left here 9 hours ago, and what their mobile phone number is.

I always know where to find the best vegetarian-kosher-Mongolian-barbecue restaurants. I know exactly what to see and do in this city in fifteen minutes without spending any money and without getting caught in traffic. I take personal blame for airline food, traffic jams, rental car flat tires, and the nation's economy.

"I am a Front Desk Agent"

I realize that you meant to book your reservation here. People often confuse us with the Galaxy Delight Motel, Antarctica. Of course I can "fit you in" and yes, you may have the special £1 rate because you are affiliated with the Hoboken Accounting and Bagel Club.

I am expected to smile, empathize, sympathize, console, condole, upsell, downsell (and know when to do which), perform, sing, dance, fix the printer, and tell your friends that you're here. And I know exactly where 613 Possum Trot Lane is in the Way Out There subdivision that they just built last week.

After all, I AM a Front Desk Agent!

Before we begin

Okay, before we get started you should know that you may need some materials whilst reading this book:

- A pen
- A notepad
- A voice recorder (you can usually download an app for your phone, or use a Dictaphone... basically anything to record your voice!)

Before beginning your read please take a few minutes to write down what tasks you will complete and skills you will need on a daily basis in your role. Think about everything you do and all the times you interact with people.

Your Role

This book is all about your role as a receptionist, front of house assistant, greeting clerk – in fact whatever your title is, if you work in a role that is customer facing within a hotel you will make good use of this book.

You would already have thought of many different things that make up your role in your earlier exercise; however here is what I advise to be some of the tasks you will complete on a daily basis:

- Check guests in/out
- Enter reservations
- Deal with telephone enquiries
- Transfer calls to other departments
- Sign for and check all deliveries
- Handle cash, and other safe deposits
- Deal with requests for local information
- Deal with guest queries and complaints
- Co-ordinate with management and sales for functions and events
- Deal with conference delegate registrations and conference organiser requests
- Arrange dinner bookings
- Upsell meals and in-house services to guests
- Process faxes, emails and letters
- Process deposits, payments and generate bills
- Administer signage and other information for the front desk
- Clean the front of house area
- Arrange for coffee stations and other items to be refreshed
- Update room availability on certain websites
- Arrange maintenance repairs

Your Role

- Complete courtesy calls to guests
- Program electronic keys and sign in/out hard keys
- Complete regular reservation checks
- Liaise with all departments to enhance guest experience

This seems like a lot of work for one shift! However within a few days, you will soon be putting all the pieces together and smoothly doing all the above, without even realising!

We know what tasks you will be doing and we will look at some of these in more depth later on, but now we need to think about the skills you will be using on a daily basis.

The main skills you will use are:

- **Interpersonal** – liaising with guests, colleagues and management to ensure smooth running of the entire hotel
- **Organisation** – a key feature of working on Front of House is the ability to be well organised at all times
- **Negotiation** – whether it is handling a complaint, or selling a room, you will often need to negotiate with others to get the best possible outcome for all parties
- **Call handling** – a lot of business comes from telephone enquiries, and a lot of complaints are handled over the phone as well; so how you handle the call is crucial
- **Sales** – a key part of any customer facing role, you should be utilising every opportunity to increase revenue across the hotel
- **I.T** – a lot of work is computerised, so you will need to be adept at using the computer systems in place, and use them in accordance with company guidelines to retain consistency

Your Role

- **Multi-tasking** – you will often need to multitask, be it using the computer whilst on the phone, or checking a guest in whilst directing them to their room

Did you come up with any more than this? You may well have done because there are a multitude of skills that you use on a daily basis to fulfil your role.

Key Note:
Even though you will use multiple skills, it is important to use them effectively. For example, it would not be wise to multi-task and deal with reservations whilst also handling a complaint, and neither would you over-use your sales skills and seem 'pushy' to guests.

Interpersonal Skills

This section will discuss the way in which you interact with other people in 2 separate categories – Colleagues and Guests.

Colleagues

When you work with people and work within a team, you sometimes find it hard at first to 'fit in'. This can be daunting and frightening to some; however you need to remember that everyone has been through the same experience when they first started!

You may find that there are people in your team or hotel that you get on with better than others; this is perfectly natural – human nature is not designed to suit everyone, and each person has their own personality and preferences.

You must remember above all, to remain professional at all times. How you feel towards someone can be interpreted fairly easily from your vocal tone, mannerisms, body language and what you actually say.

Let's take a look at a fairly common statement that you may hear (say this in your head):

"Can you enter this reservation for me please?"

Normally, people will react with an 'affirmative' (positive) response, but surely your response depends on how something has been stated to you in the first place?

Think about where the tone and emphasis is placed in the sentence.

Interpersonal Skills

If the emphasis was on "*can*", how would it make you feel? Probably you would feel as though your ability is being questioned as the emphasis is on whether or not you are able to do the task.

Now how about if the emphasis was on "*you*"? This may make you feel more important and trusted as the emphasis is about you personally completing the task.

What if the emphasis was on "*please*"? Depending on the tone, you may feel belittled by the request, or that the person requesting the task is pleading with you.

This is not definitive, it is to help you realise just how important it is to place the emphasis correctly within sentences to avoid making requests or statements that could be misinterpreted. Let's take a look at how others can interpret what you say....

How would you feel if someone said that you were rude to them? Would you think you were rude to them? Even though you were as nice as possible to them?

Let's take a statement and look at how it could be interpreted:
> "*Unfortunately, I can't do that because I will not have the time*"

If this was said as nicely as possible and in as fair a manner as possible how could it be rude? The truth is that regardless of how you say something, or how it was intended, if the person you are saying it to perceives the statement as rude, then it *is* rude.

Interpersonal Skills

Sound strange? How could something not intended as rude, *be* rude? The answer is simple, as the resulting effect does not stem from intent or delivery; it is caused by the interpretation by the recipient.

So how can we stop ourselves from being misinterpreted? There is no 'magic bullet'; you have to rely on the entire set-up of the conversation. You need to ensure that when you are declining a request or saying something that *potentially* could be construed as negative (e.g. "I can't do that" or "Unfortunately, that is not possible") you must ensure that you do not emphasise the 'negative' word in the sentence (such as those underlined).

Key Note:

Above all else, you must be professional with your colleagues. This means that, even if you do not like someone you work with, you must still acknowledge them, work with them and co-operate with them. Failing to do so will cause more friction than is necessary. If you have a genuine complaint about someone's behaviour, this should be brought to the attention of your manager and examples provided so that this may be dealt with professionally.

You should also extend your professionalism to those colleagues who are your friends outside of work. Whilst it is encouraged to enjoy yourself at work, you should always be aware that guests could be within earshot of your conversation (and usually they will not be too interested in what you did last night), so where possible, keep it professional! This also helps to reduce conflicts in work because of incidents that happen outside of work (imagine the atmosphere if you fell out as friends then had to work a shift together – keeping it professional inside work will reduce tension).

Finally, and this is common sense but sometimes people need reminding – NEVER swear at a colleague or use nicknames for colleagues whilst in areas that guests can access or hear you.

Interpersonal Skills

Guests

A lot of this section will be common sense, and I will try to avoid insulting your intelligence for as much of this area as possible.

There are some core statements that I want to share with you that have helped me in understanding guest interaction and how to deal with the majority of clientele:

1. Each guest is unique

No two guests are the same, even if they are twins! Everyone differs in how they interact with you, other guests and the hotel as a whole and you should never try to treat 2 guests as the same – doing so will make the guest feel undervalued and unappreciated. You should use different phrases with different guests and try to maintain a personal touch with each guest. If you have standard greetings or check-in/out speeches that people follow word for word, GET RID OF THEM NOW!

I cannot stress how important it is to avoid 'cookie cutter' speeches when interacting with guests. You may have had previous training that says you should always greet a guest with 'Hello, welcome to Hotel A' or similar and this phrase is fine for the first time guest, but begins to wear thin for long term or regular guests.

To put this in to context, think about something that annoys a lot of people – automated telephone menu systems! What happens when you hear the menu? Do you switch off or listen intently just to realise that the option you needed was the first one that was given? You either know what is going to be said, or you have listened to what seems like irrelevant information and wasted your time. That is how a guest may feel if they have stayed in hotels

Interpersonal Skills

regularly, which renders your speech redundant and in turn can be just plain annoying to the guest!

Write down below how you currently greet a guest:

_____
_____
_____
_____
_____
_____
_____

If possible, record yourself saying it 5 times, and play it back to yourself, or just say the statement out loud 5 times in a row, listening intently to yourself.

Now answer these questions:

How does it make you feel? (Probably a bit weird hearing your own voice, but think beyond that – did it make you feel happy? Bored? Anxious?)

_____
_____
_____
_____

What tones were used? Was it upbeat and energetic? Was it flat and boring? Did it change and get more boring the more you heard it?

_____
_____
_____
_____

Interpersonal Skills

How could you vary what you say? What could you do or say differently? Write down at least 3 different ways of greeting a guest (it may help to think about the different types of guest you meet – one greeting for leisure guests, one for conference guests, one for business guests etc).

_____

_____

_____

_____

_____

_____

_____

We will work on the greetings in more depth later in the book. This exercise has just been designed to get you thinking about how you sound to a guest at one of the most crucial times – arrival!

2. Every guest has the right to have high expectations of you

We have all met them – the people who 'look down on you' or who expect you to do everything and 'spoon-feed' them.

Sometimes you may find guests condescending, or downright rude, so what do you do about it? The answer is simple….nothing! Remain non-reactive to the situation. By doing so you will not give away any signals to an aggressive or emotive person that could be misread or misinterpreted, by being calm and responding in a polite way, you are less likely to become emotionally guarded or aggressive to the guest, and the guest is more likely to become politer towards you – so here is a first golden nugget to remember: **Behaviour Breeds behaviour!** If you are aggressive to a guest, they will be aggressive in response; if you are friendly and helpful to a guest, they will (usually) be the same in return.

Interpersonal Skills

No matter how frustrating, or obnoxious you may find a guest, you should never let them know this is how you feel about them, neither should you openly discuss their behaviour in public areas.

We will talk some more later about how guests think and what drives them to behave in the way they do, but remember that ultimately, that guest is paying for you to be employed – without guests there is no money for the hotel, which means no hotel and no role for you!

3. Every guest has the right to complain

No matter how trivial, a guest will complain because they feel it is necessary to do so. Later on I will cover complaint handling in more depth, especially challenging your perception of complaints.

All you need to remember is, despite how you may feel, every guest has the basic right to complain about elements of their stay.

4. Each guest is your boss

This may seem confusing; surely your manager is your boss? Not strictly true – your manager delegates roles and tasks to you, but it is the guest who actually dictates the majority of your role. Sometimes guests may seemingly 'overstep the mark' and become extremely bossy or blunt towards you, sometimes they will be your best friend, but they are 'master and commander' of you for their stay.

So there we have the 4 statements that should become your 'mantra'. To summarise these points:

Every guest is unique, has high expectations as your boss and has the right to tell you if they are unhappy!

Interpersonal Skills

Organisation

A messy desk represents a messy mind – a common phrase that many people have heard; I don't believe this is true – many people like an 'organised chaos' to work in, but how does this look to a guest?

How would you feel if you walked in to a hotel and saw a messy, disorganised desk? Write down what this represents to you – what do you think will be the guests impression if they saw you surrounded by paperwork and files when they arrived?

_____
_____
_____
_____
_____

Is this the kind of impression that you want to be giving to the guest? Is it the kind of impression your manager or the hotel owner wants to give to the guest?

One important thing to think of is how you think a hotel reception should look. Write down what you think are the key things that should be noticeable about a hotel reception; include what impression the reception should give to you – think about your own hotel and the impression you want your guests to have.

_____
_____
_____
_____
_____

Interpersonal Skills

Being organised is partially about knowing where everything is at a given time. On the following page, draw a simple diagram of your work area, as though you are looking down on your reception (only draw your desk/working space and back office behind the desk (if you have one). Label as many places as you can on the diagram to indicate where items are. Label at least the following (if they are used in your hotel):

- Archive (old registration cards from departed guests)
- Registration Cards (arriving guests)
- PC's/workstations
- Reservation backup (confirmations/booking documents)
- Handover Diary
- Local Information
- Fax and Phone
- Banking/receipts storage
- Safe
- Paper and other stationery
- Visitors signing in/out book

These things may be in multiple places, or may change location regularly, for these items you should mark where they are normally kept.

You may find this harder than you first thought – also draw and label anything not listed above – how many items can you remember the location of?

My Reception Desk:

Negotiation

This has little place elsewhere in this book (except for complaint handling), so I will cover the majority of negotiation skills here.

Once I heard someone say that 'compromise is for people who are wrong' and I thought this to be extremely interesting. Mainly because compromise is something we all have to do on a daily basis, but does it mean that everyone is always wrong?

Negotiation is about reaching a compromise. The Oxford English Dictionary defines negotiation as:

> 'Discussion aimed at reaching an agreement'

And compromise is defined as:

> 'An agreement or settlement of a dispute that is reached by each side making concessions'

It is worthwhile noting that neither definition states that either party 'wins' or 'loses', so if you think that negotiation or compromise is about winning or losing, this chapter will challenge that thinking.

Think about a common scenario that I am sure everyone has faced at some point (I will use Mr Smith as a reference throughout this book. He is a theoretical guest who stays in lots of hotels, has high standards and expects immaculate service at all times!)

Negotiation

Mr Smith calls to reserve a room for the evening. He has been quoted £99 for the room on a bed and breakfast basis, but his budget will not stretch to this. Write down what you would do in this situation:

_____
_____
_____
_____
_____
_____

You will probably have put one of 2 options (something similar to these):
- Stick to your guns. The rate is non-negotiable and if he wants to stay he will have to pay £99.

Or
- See if there is another lower rate we could offer him

These generally are the only 2 options available to most reception staff.

Let's turn the situation around and look at it from Mr Smith's perspective. He is presented with 2 options:
- Pay more than I can afford

Or
- Negotiate for something more in line with my budget

From either perspective, option 2 would be better – for Mr Smith it would be better to get the hotel he wants at a price he can afford, and from the hotel's perspective we have 2 different views. The hotel can get the room sold and gets revenue, or can hold out and hope that someone pays the £99 (although this is not guaranteed).

The preferable choice for both parties is to negotiate and reach a suitable compromise. You may have already noticed that the hotel has 2 views, and

Negotiation

may have wondered why this is the case. The view of selling the room for what you can is most commonly held by people who are 'risk adverse' and the opposing view of holding out hope for selling at the standard rate is normally held by those who are 'risk favourable'.

The risk to the hotel is that they could sell the room at a lower rate and potentially miss out on a booking at the higher rate, or they could not sell at a lower rate and hope that someone books at the higher rate. So before beginning any negotiation, we need to think about the risk something presents. Can you think of another risk to the hotel that has not yet been stated?

_____

_____

_____

If you thought of the risk of losing a potential guest for good (after all, if you will not negotiate rates, why would Mr Smith stay with you in the future), then well done!

So let's summarise the risks for both sides:

If we don't negotiate	If we do negotiate
Mr Smith may not book	Mr Smith will probably book
Mr Smith may never try to book with us in future	Mr Smith is more likely to book in the future (or at least enquire)
The hotel could lose revenue from a lost booking	The hotel is guaranteed revenue (albeit less than the rack rate)

One statement stands out here – the hotel is guaranteed revenue. This gives us more than enough reason to begin negotiating as on one side of the

Negotiation

argument we have no guarantees, and on the other, we have at least one guarantee!

So how do we negotiate? In just a few simple steps you can negotiate effectively and reach the best possible outcome for both parties involved (an effective compromise). The guidelines I am about to cover do not just relate to the situation outlined previously, they can actually be applied to any negotiation situation.

Key Note:
There are many books out there that will provide further information on negotiation, and I would recommend that you do your own further reading if you want to know more about the art of negotiation (which is different to persuasion!)

Stages of negotiation

There are three key stages to negotiating, the first 2 of which 'set the stage' and the final one comes naturally if stages 1 and 2 are followed correctly.

Stage 1 is to 'assess expectations'. This is where you find out what the other party is expecting.

Before I go any further on this, I wish to point out that I will refer to 'Needs and Wants' which is covered in more depth in the complaint handling section of this book, however I have put a brief explanation in here for you.

The prime difference I would like to advise you of is that a 'Need' is something that is non-negotiable. It is something that is unchanged (e.g. requiring a bedroom is a need for the guest at the moment of booking). A 'Want' is something that someone would like, but is not necessary to complete the transaction (e.g. a guest may like to have an upgrade, but this can be eliminated from their requirements as long as their 'Need' is met). So a 'Need' is something necessary and cannot be negotiated, a 'Want' can be negotiated as it is in addition to someone's needs.

So back to assessing expectations. Negotiation usually begins with one party telling the other what they need, and what they desire (most commonly in this order. E.g. a guest states they would 'like to book a room, one of the upgrades if possible'). Can you identify Mr Smith's needs in this scenario? (Hint: there are at least 2 needs he has!).

_____

_____

_____

_____

Stages of negotiation

Need 1: He needs to have a bedroom for the night
Need 2: He needs this to be within his budget.

It can safely be assumed that both are non-negotiable as he can only spend what he has available, making there the 2 needs identified above.

So the first step of any negotiation is to assess what the other person requires. This could be a mixture of needs and wants but unless you know this, you cannot begin to negotiate.

Stage 2 is to 'state your requirements and capabilities'. This sounds a bit ominous but does not mean you have to be blunt, aggressive or agitated. It is simply about stating what you can and cannot do.

Let's take Mr Smith's call again. You would need to tell him what you can and cannot do for his situation. We know he needs a room that fits his budget, and also that you are selling rooms outside of his budget. In this scenario we will assume that Mr Smith has already been advised of the room rate, and you have already discovered that his budget is £75 (because you assessed his expectations). Now we state what we can and cannot do and cover the options available.

Key Note:

As a general rule in hotels, you should never refuse a booking because the rate is too high for a guest. You should always refer to your sales/revenue/reservations/management team if you do not have the authority to amend rates.

Stages of negotiation

So we would tell him that we have the rooms, but our standard rate is £99 for bed and breakfast. But, most importantly, we advise that we will see what we can do to reach a compromise.

Simply by stating that you are willing to compromise is suggesting that you *can* do something for him, which engages him into negotiation without necessarily realising that this is taking place. Instead he is inclined to wait and see *what* you can do for him.

So we have started negotiating already, Mr Smith has told us what he wants, and we have told him what we can do. This is the point where many people end the negotiation, at no more than a stalemate with refusal of either party to relent.

We actually need to move to stage 3 now, and do so quickly!

Stage 3 is 'suggest, offer, and conclude' (making this into 3 separate stages would make it too complicated!).

You need to suggest a solution, firmly offer it, and then 'seal the deal'. To suggest a solution you need to know what you can and cannot offer. In some cases you can simply match what he wants to pay, but is this really beneficial?

I am not one for 'corporate attitude', however I have business sense. In this scenario, it would be more financially feasible to remove breakfast and charge £75 room only, than to drop the bed and breakfast rate to £75 (as there is more profit from it being room only than having to allocate a portion of the rate for the breakfast).

Stages of negotiation

So we have a potential solution, which is suggested (e.g. 'I may be able to do £75 for room only'). Note the wording – the word 'may' is used. This is because it is not making a firm offer, but is stating that it is a potential solution. If the guest agrees, you can then firmly offer it to them and confirm the booking at that rate.

Alternatively you might have to speak to your manager, in which case you would suggest that you may be able to do a special rate after speaking to your manager, and then return to the guest with a firm offer.

This stage can be complicated, it is mainly about suggesting a solution and assessing whether the guest will accept it. If they accept, make it a firm offer, get their agreement and confirm everything.

If they do not accept (e.g. he wants breakfast included), you will need to re-affirm your original suggestion to the guest to demonstrate that you are 'standing your ground'; this then becomes up to the guest to decide whether they will accept the compromise or push further to achieve what they want. Only re-affirm your original offer once – failing to back down or try another solution will only cause negotiations to cease and cause friction between both parties! If the guest 'stands their ground', try another solution (e.g. if they pay the £99 you will upgrade them).

Key Note:
Your offer should always start with only providing what is needed as you can then 'up-sell' the additional wants of the guest. If someone needs a room and has £50 to spend, offering a room for £50 is financially more feasible than offering dinner bed and breakfast for £50 – remember that by offering everything in the first offer is counterproductive; it can lead to guests demanding more for cheaper and leaves you little to actually negotiate with!

When negotiation fails

The previous steps are not the 'be all and end all' of negotiation. There are many intricacies of human nature that are not taken into account here. This is just a brief outline of very basic negotiation and a lot of it comes naturally. The main concept is that you realise that negotiation is not about someone winning or losing, it is about both parties being happy with the outcome of a situation.

Negotiations will fail, but many more will succeed! If a negotiation fails, think about why it failed – were you too stubborn? Was the guest too stubborn? The answer is usually one or the other! If you were too stubborn, think about what you could change for future scenarios; if the guest was too stubborn, think about how you might have otherwise have fulfilled their needs.

Call handling

Dealing with telephone enquiries is a staple part of the receptionist role, and some days you feel more like a call centre operative than a receptionist! No matter how many calls you take it a day, be it 5, 50 or even 500, every call should be opened in the same way.

Like a good story, the call should be properly constructed with a beginning, middle and an end – hopefully it will be a happy ending!

So let's start with the beginning. Many people think that call handling begins with answering the phone, but this is a common misconception. Call handling actually begins far before this. Imagine being taught how to write but never being taught what a pen or pencil was – this would render the training useless as you would not have the basic skill of knowing how to use the equipment, so before we begin talking about how to handle calls, write down how to carry out the basic functions below (if available at your property):

Make a call:

Answer a call:

End a call:

Transfer a call to someone else:

Place someone on hold:

Call handling

Hopefully you will have been able to do this. If you do not know how to do this, or have not yet started your role, you should ensure this is one of the first things you learn in your role, and write down the details in the spaces given so you can refer to them in future if needed.

We have worked out now how to use the phone in your premises, so we are already part way there for dealing with the call. Some would say the hardest part is over because as soon as you answer that call, you are committed into a conversation.

Greeting the Call

What would you say to greet the guest to your hotel? Write down what you would say when answering the telephone to an external call:

_____

_____

_____

_____

_____

Before going any further, I would like to state that there is no 'right or wrong answer' to how you should answer a call. There is my idea of best practice, but you may have differing standards within your hotel. Whilst you should always adhere to your own hotel's policies and procedures, if you think they can be improved after reading this section, discuss this with your manager (or implement changes if you are the manager).

Call handling

When answering the phone, I have 2 standard greetings that I use, dependant on the circumstances (For the purpose of this book, both you and I will be working for the Pillow Inn):

> "Good Morning/Afternoon/Evening, welcome to Pillow Inn, you're speaking to Matt, how may I help?"

Or, if the caller has been waiting for more than 3 rings

> "Good Morning/Afternoon/Evening, sorry to keep you waiting, you are through to Matt at Pillow Inn, how may I help?"

You may have similar versions of this that are used in your hotel, but let's take a look at why I use these phrases.

Firstly, they sound fairly natural; it is difficult to make them sound forced. Secondly, they also sound professional, but friendly.

I am not going to dictate how to answer the phone, as the greeting varies from hotel to hotel. You should find a greeting that suits you and is natural to you, there is nothing worse than being greeted by someone who says a stock phrase through gritted teeth or sounds robotic. I will however lay down a few ground rules for your opening:

Rule 1 – Do not make it too informal.

Saying 'Hi' is too informal to be used when answering the phone to potential clientele. 'Hi' is a shortened form of 'Hello' and, personally, it makes me think that if you cannot be bothered to say the full word 'Hello', then how bothered are you about providing me with a good call?

Call handling

Rule 2 – Always state your name and that of your hotel

When greeting someone on the phone, you need to start building a connection straight away, and one way to get this started is to introduce yourself by name; the caller then also has a point of reference should they call back. By stating the name of the hotel, the guest will immediately know that they have contacted the correct place.

Rule 3 – Always be prepared for the call

We have covered how to answer the phone, but what do you do when the phone is ringing? This all depends on what you were doing when the phone started ringing – do you finish off your current task or drop everything to answer the phone? Either way, you still need to do the same thing – be ready to take the call. This literally takes one second and is extremely easy – stop, take a breath and answer the phone, it really is that simple! If you do not do this, you will probably sound flustered or agitated when you answer the phone, which is not a good impression to give!

So, to the middle...

The types of call you receive will vary; from complex requests for historic bills and accounting details, multiple bookings and local information or directions, through to simple calls such as asking for the address and being put through to another extension

Let's start with an easy one – putting someone through to another extension. The first things to be aware of is how to do this on your phone system. For some systems you can simply dial the extension number and hang up, for others you will need to engage in a conference call; I am not going to tell

Call handling

you the specifics of every single phone system out there, as quite frankly it would get rather boring.

So what about what we say to the callers? There are two methods of transfer that are adopted; blind and introduced transfer.

Blind Transfer

A 'Blind' transfer is when the caller is not introduced; they are just transferred straight through to the extension they requested, without any introduction to the person they are calling. These are fairly straightforward, but you should never transfer someone through without telling the caller you are going to transfer them (imagine if you were put on hold during a call without being told – this is in effect the same thing!). To tell someone you are transferring them, you can adopt any phrase from the basic 'I will transfer you now' through to the more professional 'If you would please hold, I will transfer you through to extension XXX now'.

From this point forward you have 2 outcomes; either the call will be picked up by the person on that extension (or their voicemail), or the call will revert back to you as it has been unanswered. If the call is picked up or goes to voicemail, there is nothing you can do... or is there?

The picky amongst you may have noticed that at the beginning of this section, I stated nothing about getting the caller's name. This is recommended for two separate reasons; firstly if the call is introduced (which we cover in a moment) you will need this information but more importantly, if the call is not answered and bounces back, or goes to voicemail, and then the caller rings back again, you can pre-empt any issues and stop any complaint.

Call handling

Let's look at a scenario: you call a hotel and ask to be put through to sales. There is no answer and you leave a message. You don't receive a call so ring back in a couple of hours, and the same thing happens. By the third call, you would be a bit annoyed and it is now the responsibility of the person putting you through to the sales office to ensure that you can speak to someone.

From a receptionist's point of view, if you knew the same caller had tried repeatedly without success, the question in your mind should be whether you should try contacting someone yourself to get the call dealt with quickly, or whether you should try alternative means of contact such as emailing sales. I have regularly wandered around a hotel to find people to pass on a message and get someone a call back; remember that a lost call is potentially lost revenue! Although you may not have to do it often, if you receive a message to call someone, then call them... quickly!

If you encounter a similar situation to this, simply advise the caller 'I believe you have called a few times, has anyone dealt with your query?' The caller will either say yes or no, but they will be thankful either way that you have recognised that they have called a few times – again this confirms the opening of the call by making them feel welcome. If they say no, ask them for a contact number and advise them you will try to get hold of the person they need an alternative way, something like 'If I can take a contact number, what I will do is go and find someone from that team to give you a call back as soon as possible' will usually suffice.

Key Note:
Always ensure that call back requests are followed up! If you cannot do this yourself, ask someone else to do it as a priority on your behalf.

Call handling

Introduced Transfers

Introduced transfers work in a similar way; except that you will be introducing the call to the person you are transferring the caller to. In this case, you would advise the caller that you are going to transfer them (as stated previously) and also let the person you are calling know who is calling (and if required by your hotel, what the query is regarding). Some people find this difficult, particularly as asking why someone is calling can be perceived by some as rude (remember us talking about perceptions of what is said). The key is to ask simple questions; usually 'can I take your name and what the call is regarding?' is perfectly acceptable for most establishments. For those who want a more professional method, a preferred way of stating this might be 'If I could take your name and the reason for your call, I will transfer your call to the appropriate person to deal with your enquiry'.

Despite saying this, there is no 'hard and fast rule' for how to deal with transferring calls. As an experiment why not try ringing a few of your competitors to enquire about the packages they have advertised, or room rates etc. and take notes on how your call was dealt with and what was said. If your phone has the capability, it may be worthwhile recording the call as well so you can listen back to it. You should make note of the following:

- What was said
- How did the call make you feel (did you feel welcome? Did you feel as though the call was rushed?)
- What impression did you get from the call (did you get an image of a professional, caring hotel, or one that was not that interested in dealing with you?)
- How would you have changed/improved the call?
- What will you implement or change about how you handle calls as a result of this call?

Call handling

> **Key Note:**
> If the guest has already stated their name and reason for calling, do not ask them to repeat it; this can be very annoying as you should have been ready for the call and prepared to listen! Similarly if the caller asks for a specific person, transfer them directly to that person.

Reservation Enquiries

Reservation enquiries should be dealt with as per your own internal policies. If one does not exist you should use the following framework:

Ask the caller for the dates they would like to stay and what type of room, or rooms, they would like to book.

> "I will just check availability for you. Could you confirm the date you are looking to book? And could you also confirm the type of room you are looking for?"

Check availability and confirm the available rates for the date requested.
- If there is no availability, either offer to 'waitlist' the reservation (if implemented within your hotel) or ask if there any other dates you can check.

> "It doesn't appear that we have any availability at the moment for that date. Are there any alternative dates I can check for you?"

> If 'No' – "Would you like me to put your reservation on to our waiting list and then we can call you to confirm if we have any cancellations?"

- If only the requested room type is unavailable, but other room types are, offer them a different room type to accommodate their needs.

Call handling

"There isn't any availability for a [room type] room, but we do have some [alternative room type] rooms available if you would like for me to get the rates for these instead"

- If the guest sounds unsure about the rate, ask the caller what budget they are working to and speak to your manager or reservations/sales team to check if you can sell at a lower rate. Then offer the lower rate to the caller (if approved).

"If you let me know what budget you are working to, I will see if I can get a lower rate for you"

Enter the reservation on to the system, remembering to get at least 2 different forms of contact (e.g. mobile number and email address). Confirm the booking to the guest, detailing at least the dates, room type, board basis and rate, along with any special requests.

"Okay, so just to confirm, that is booked for you for arrival on [date] for [no nights] nights. You have reserved a [room type] for [no adults] adults (and [no children] children) at a rate of [rate] on a [board basis] basis. [Confirm any special requests such as confirming the number of cots or temporary beds, along with any table bookings for dinner etc.]"

Key Note:
Always ask a guest if they would like to take a note of their reservation confirmation number now, and also offer to send confirmation via email (if they have email access). As always, follow up on this and make sure confirmation is sent if requested.

Ending the call

Always finish on a positive note. There are two standard ends to a call that I use, and these can be adapted or modified to suit your circumstances.

For reservations

"That is all finalised for you, is there anything else I can help you with? (Usually the response is no, but answer any questions the guest may have). I look forward to seeing you on [arrival date]. Thank you for your call, goodbye."

For general enquiries

"Thank you for your call, I hope you have a good day, goodbye"

Now some of you will have thought that the last version for general enquiries was a bit cheesy. I personally think it makes the ending of the call a bit brighter and often modify this. For example if someone has had a bad day, I will 'hope their day gets better', or if they were a complainant I will thank them for taking the time to talk to me about the issues they encountered and 'I hope everything has now been resolved for you'.

Key Note:
It is important to provide the same service over the telephone as you would when dealing with someone face to face. You cannot put someone 'on hold' when they are in front of you, therefore avoid placing callers on hold unless absolutely necessary (i.e. to check with a colleague). When you do put someone on hold, never do so for more than 30 seconds without going back to the caller confirm that you are still looking into the situation. To demonstrate how long 30 seconds is, look at a clock or watch in silence and see how long 30 seconds actually is. Now imagine what it would be like if you had been put on hold for longer than that!

Sales Skills

There is no such thing as the 'perfect salesperson'. Many people may profess to be the best at selling, but are they managing to sell to everyone they try to sell to? The answer will always be no! There are many of you who, like me, will say that selling is not a receptionist's job – that's what they have sales teams for. I agree with you... partially!

On reception, you are as responsible for generating revenue for the property as any other department; in fact you are probably the only department (aside from Food and Beverage) that has the opportunity to make instant revenue. Sales make future revenue (money that we will receive several days, weeks or months down the line), but reception makes the revenue there and then – if you sell an upgrade, it is usually to a guest checking in or arriving in the next couple of days; if you sell breakfast or dinner, it is normally to guests in-house that day.

The one thing I do want to make clear is that sales are NOT the be all and end all of reception. Any manager reading this that believes that reception should be selling continuously needs to take a step back and realise all the other things that reception do. I agree that sales can be targeted as an incentive, but not as a priority – your priority should ALWAYS be guest experience/customer care, sales comes about 4th or 5th on my priority list; targets are set for my teams and incentives run regularly, but no-one is derided for not selling, only ever pulled up for not even trying. I only ever push sales hard when revenue is low and the business needs every penny, but I do not turn my team into walking, talking sales machines!

I want to give you a really common example of a potential sale that many receptionists fail to do anything with. Mr Smith checks out. During the check-

Sales Skills

out he states that he had a really nice stay and will look at staying again in the future.

Now, to many of you this will be something you hear regularly, but do little about. It only takes 2 seconds to ask whether there are any dates Mr Smith would like you to check for availability. The guest will not be offended, in fact most are the opposite and are glad to be offered; it saves them the hassle of making a phone call later on! And yes, it really can be that simple! Not very often do people book there and then, and if they don't want to book now, simply offer the hotels direct telephone number and invite the guest to call when they want to book and you will get them the best possible rate. If the guest stayed on a promotional offer, suggest taking their email address so you can email them future offers. This rule applies to any suggestion that the guest makes, no matter how subtle. For example, a guest checks in and asks what time the restaurant is open – why not offer to show them the menu, or sell them the set menu (if you have one). If they say they are here for an anniversary celebration, offer a room upgrade and wine to their room, and/or dinner in the restaurant, or even breakfast in bed.

The point I am trying to make is that there are opportunities to sell at almost every turn, you just have to realise what opportunities there are. When you are next on shift, keep a tally of how many times you hear a guest enquiring about something within the hotel as they check in, or how many say they had a great time on check-out – these are the most commonly missed opportunities. Some days you will have 50 or more such opportunities, on other days you will have only 3 or 4.

Now look at your tally and think about how many were actually offered something in response to their query. If you have a low 'query to offer' ratio (how many queries there were compared to how many offers were actually made), you need to start promoting more when the opportunities arise.

Sales Skills

To sell is really easy, you have an opportunity for at least 3 different sales on check-in; breakfast, dinner and a room upgrade (if they have not been purchased already!) It really is as simple as asking the guest. If you form this as part of your check-in procedure (as we will discuss later), it comes naturally and will not sound forced in any way.

There is nothing I can say that will make you sell more. Again there are loads of books and reference sources out there to help with sales, and no doubt someone you know will be able to help you out. The key is remembering to ask at every available opportunity. This even extends beyond check-in and departure.

If you are a conference venue and you hear guests talking about arranging rooms for the evening, if you know you have rooms to sell, politely advise them that you have availability and offer to speak to sales or the conference organiser to arrange a negotiated rate for them for the evening. They will often be thankful as then they do not need to worry about travelling around to find a hotel or to get to and from the venue. Similarly, you could really help with room sales if you have rooms but know other hotels in the area are full – simply ring and let them know you have rooms if they need any (we will talk about out-booking situations later); this is particularly useful if you are near any airports or ferry terminals!

I.T Skills

Most people have basic computer skills, but time invested in improving these is more than worthwhile. There are literally hundreds of website and resources that can help you brush up on computer skills; I am not talking about how to fully re-design a program or create fully animated websites, but merely about knowing how to use common programs you use at work, such as spreadsheet and word processing software programs.

The basic I.T skill (beyond the very basics) is knowing how to use your computer system for reservations and availability. You should know at least the following core things:

- How to check availability
- How to enter a reservation
- How to process a payment
- How to check a guest in
- How to check a guest out

This is only 6 things you NEED to know and you should be confident at doing these before undertaking these tasks alone. If you think you need further assistance, refer to your manager, trainer or a colleague for further help.

Key Note:

I believe the best way to learn is through teaching others. Think about the common things you do on your computer system (such as those previously mentioned), and write down a step-by-step guide of how to do them. Try doing it without being at the computer, only using the system if you really get stuck. For this exercise you must be committed to doing as much as you can without referring to training materials or the actual system itself. If you miss anything, simply try again; I do not expect it to be perfect first time, but if you got at least 75% of it right without looking at the system, you can be confident you know what you are doing!

Once you have done this, why not type it up – it could be a handy guide for other new employees (if you do not have one already).

Multitasking

As a receptionist you need to act like a juggler, always keeping multiple things moving at once, such as entering a reservation whilst dealing with telephone enquiries and giving keys to staff, whilst keeping an eye on the fax machine and getting people to sign in and out. Sound stressful? The easiest way to deal with these is to not overburden yourself; if you have a queue of guests, ring someone to come and help (guests rarely mind this); if you have people at the desk and are in the middle of a conversation on the phone, simply acknowledging the guest will work wonders and they will happily (usually) wait for you to finish.

Key Note:

Regardless of what you are doing, guests take priority! If the phone rings whilst you have a guest at the desk, before answering the phone, ask the guest if it is okay for you to answer the call; I have never had a guest say no! If you are doing something else and a guest comes to the desk, acknowledge the waiting guest and deal with them as a priority, over what you are doing – if you are on the phone, ask the caller if they are okay to be placed on hold for a short time and you will come back to them.

I will not tell you how to prioritise, as this is down to individual preference, but to me, the guest at the desk takes precedence at all times! Although I am never shy of answering the phone if it is ringing and someone is talking to me – as long as you are polite and confirm that the interruption to your conversation is okay then you are remaining professional!

Most people understand when you are busy – in their jobs they have probably had a similar day at some point! The key to multi-tasking' is to actually not 'multi-task' at all! Simply do one task at a time. Keep a list of

Multitasking

jobs to do if necessary (we will discuss shift checklists later on); trying to do too many things at once leads to errors, so take a deep breath, think about what you are doing and then tackle all your jobs one by one!

So this concludes the first section on skills needed to be a receptionist. There are probably many more skills that could be added to this, but I do not want to work too much on these as they are skills that you will pick up as your time as a receptionist increases; they will also be mentioned throughout the remaining chapters.

Let's go now through the 'guest journey'; from searching for a hotel, right through to departing. There are hundreds of 'interaction points' along the way (times at which a member of staff speaks to or sees the guest).

The Guest Journey

Think about when you last stayed in a hotel; where did your interaction with the hotel begin? Most people think it is at the time of phoning the hotel to check availability or similar, but your actual guest journey starts well before this.

Each guest that stays with you has made a conscious decision to do so, and in the modern world of review sites, tweeting and posting on peoples walls, there are now hundreds of ways that your guest interacts with the hotel, without actually speaking to a member of staff.

Driving the decision

So, what drives a decision to stay in a particular venue? There is no definitive answer to this as different people are driven by different things; some will decide purely based on a flashy website or marketing campaign, others will be because the rooms are cheap, others because the rooms are expensive! But there is one thing that is more powerful than most – word of mouth. One guest's experience can either get you more business, or get people turning away from your hotel. One bad review may not necessarily be the downfall of a hotel, but consistently bad reviews will not do you any favours. For example, many people look to review sites in order to gauge what a hotel is like before staying there, and it is up to you as a receptionist to ensure that you are not 'stoking the fire' of negative reviews by being brash, rude or insensitive.

How do you avoid the bad reviews? There is nothing I can say that will stop you from ever receiving a bad review, but what you must do is minimise the risk of a bad review; even the worst situations can be recovered from, and we will discuss this more in the complaint handling section. What is equally

The Guest Journey

important is how you deal with a bad review; most sites have the ability to post a management response, so if you spot a bad review, or any negative feedback, you will need to try and locate the details the guest (usually their experience will be noted in a handover diary or similar) and pass this over to a member of management to arrange a response to the guest. We will discuss responses a bit more in depth when we look at complaint handling later.

A bed review will not stop someone staying in a hotel; I have stayed in hotels and had really bad experiences, despite every review being positive. I have also stayed in really good hotels that have had their fair share of bad reviews! The point I am making is that every review and experience is subjective to each individual guest; no two guests will ever have exactly the same experience, so neither should every guest be treated in the same way. As I said before, each guest is unique and because of this you need to ensure that each experience they have, be it good or bad, is unique!

Our guest journey has started; they have researched the hotel and decided they want to stay with you. Now comes the booking (which is usually by phone, email or internet portal). The hardest ones to deal with are via internet portal, as you do not control any part of this; the guest is in full control of their booking, so how do you interact with them? The most important thing with internet bookings is that you understand how they work. Have a look at your own booking system and 2 or 3 sites that are used for booking with your hotel – do you know every step of the booking process? Chances are you do not but you should try and familiarise yourself with the process, so that you can at least help if a guest calls with issues over booking online. For this reason, you should always know what rate codes are used for online bookings (if you are a large enough venue to have rate codes), and how to enter a reservation on to your own booking system should something go wrong with an online booking system.

Email Bookings

Email bookings can be tricky, mainly because you usually have to send several emails back and forth, with usually some considerable delay between emails being sent and a response being received from the guest, but remember that once you have quoted a rate, you should stick to it!

Emails can be difficult to get right, and a lot of companies use standard templates for emails. Whilst these are useful, they should only ever be used as a guideline as simply copy-pasting a template and amending it is very impersonal, and the guest will get this impression. You should try to allow your own 'flair' to come forward as well as maintaining professionalism.

When responding to an email, you should always respond within 1 hour, detailing everything the guest requires, along with any further information you need to complete the booking. Here are some 'golden rules' of email writing that you should follow:

- Always refer to the guest as they refer to themselves in the email signature. If they state 'Mr J Smith', refer to them as 'Mr Smith'; if they sign the email from 'John' refer to them as 'John'. For clarity, always use their surname if provided.
- Answer all the questions put forward in the email. If the guest requests availability and rates, then provide them with these details as a bare minimum.
- Always use a spell checker and read the email back to yourself before sending! There is nothing worse than an email that refers to you by the wrong name, or uses bad English!
- Never use slang phrases or 'street terms'. This even extends to the opening and closing of an email; a golden rule is to never use 'Hi' for the first email to a guest, for the second email onwards it is generally

The Guest Journey

acceptable but only if you are on first name terms with the guest and the guest has replied with 'hi'.
- Always include an email signature with your name, role, hotel name and contact details as a bare minimum.
- Never ask a guest for credit card details via email, always ask them to ring you with the details. If they voluntarily email their card details, always ensure you print the email then delete it, along with crossing through the card details on the printed email so no-one can see them - except the last 4 digits and the expiry date. If you reply to an email that has card details on it, always replace the first 12 digits of the card with an 'X' (i.e. xxxx xxxx xxxx 1234). This prevents the card details from being used by anyone who is not authorised (ensure you have put the card details on their reservation though!)

Key Note:

With Internet and telephone bookings, it is always worthwhile ringing the guest 7 days before arrival to ensure everything is correct. This is also a chance to upsell any additional packages such as breakfast, dinner or room upgrades. Remember that with telephone and direct internet bookings, there is usually little information to back up the booking, so you need to contact the guest to ensure everything is accurate.

So now the guest has made their reservation and they are preparing to arrive. This means that you should also be preparing for their arrival.

The Guest Journey

Pre-arrival Checks

Every hotel should be operating with pre-arrival checks in place. If you do not currently have pre-arrival checks, you need to start implementing them now, as failing to do so will lead to huge headaches!

Most pre-arrival checks are carried out on a 1/3/7 day basis, meaning that if you were doing your checks today, you would check tomorrow's arrivals, arrivals for 3 days' time and arrivals for 7 days' time. So if the date was the 1st, you would check all arrivals for the 2nd, 4th and 8th.

There are several things that you will need to check, according to the system you use and the set-up in your hotel. There may be more checks that you do already, or that you can add to the following list, but here are the most basic checks that should be done:

- **Rates**
    o Are the reservations at the correct rate?
    o Are the reservations on the correct rate code for their stay? (if used at your hotel)
    o Does the rate match the booking confirmation or agreed rate?
    o Does the rate match the room type requested?

- **Deposits**
    o Have deposits for non-refundable reservations been taken?
    o Does a deposit need to be taken? (Usually deposits should only be processed for promotional rates and advance booking rates. Guests on flexible rates or those with a 'day of arrival' cancellation policy normally do not need deposits processing)
    o Have the deposits been assigned to the guest's reservation?

- o Is the deposit for the correct amount? (Including optional extras such as set price dinner menu, flowers or wine in the room etc.)

- **Guest information**
    - o Are the names formatted correctly (i.e. Capital letters for the first letter of the forename and surname)?
    - o Is the guest a VIP? Should they be upgraded?

- **Room information**
    - o Is the guest's room type correct? (Take into account the number of adults/children in the room)

- **Additional Requests**
    - o Has the guest requested any extra beds or cots for the room? (If so, does housekeeping know?)
    - o Has the guest requested any additional packages or add-ons? (E.g. purchasing breakfast/dinner, flowers in room etc.)

- **Pass on Information**
    - o What information needs to be passed to other departments?

There may be additional checks you complete on top of these for data integrity purposes, such as ensuring that travel agent details are loaded and booking references are commented in to the booking etc.

The checks that you should implement are not designed to hinder your role and just 'give you something to do'; they are there to make your role a lot easier. Imagine if you were dealing with guests continually disputing the rate or room type they have. This is a common occurrence when pre-arrival checks are not done, or are done incorrectly!

The Guest Journey

Think about how you would feel if you arrived at a hotel to find that you had not been given the room type you requested, or that you had not received the rate you expected!

Routing

Some properties use 'routing' of charges (where a specific charge or group of charges are separated to another guest's bill, a separate bill for the same guest, or to a master account). Where possible you should always apply the routing when doing pre-arrival checks. When routing charges, most systems ask you to select specific charges to be routed and where they are being routed to; always check that these details are correct. Routing of the charges makes the departure process a lot easier for the staff and guest for many reasons – can you name a few reasons why routing is useful?

You may have come up with some or more of the following:

- Ease of departure. This is probably the most important reason. By routing charges correctly, you can easily tell what a guest actually has to pay. For example, a guest who booked through a travel agent, where that travel agent is paying for the accommodation, may have had food and drink charges posted to their room. By routing charges correctly, the guests will have a bill ready for them that shows just the food and drink costs they have to pay and not the rate you have received from the travel agent for the booking.
- Streamlined procedures. Routing charges means that you do not have to manually transfer charges between accounts
- Account integrity. By routing charges you can ensure that the charges raised to an account are accurate and correct.

The Guest Journey

> **Key Note:**
> You should always ensure you only route the appropriate charges that the agent or company that will be paying have agreed to pay. For example, routing all food and drink charges is not appropriate when the company or agent is only paying for £30 worth of food and drink. Many systems allow you to put a limit in place, so that the guest pays anything over their limit.

Allocating rooms

Most hotels operate in one of 2 ways, either allocating rooms in advance, or allocating on arrival. From a Front of House perspective it is usually easier to allocate rooms on arrival, as you can then allocate rooms to guests as they become available as cleaned by housekeeping. From housekeeping and other department's perspective, it is usually easier for them if rooms are allocated in advance. Why do you think it would be useful for housekeeping to have rooms allocated in advance?

_____
_____
_____
_____
_____
_____

Allocating in advance easier for housekeeping so that they know all the following information:

- Where to place additional beds or cots
- Which guests are VIP's for additional extras such as fruit in the room
- Which rooms will be in use each day so they can staff appropriately
- Which rooms are going to be arriving early so they can prepare these first

The Guest Journey

You may have come up with more or less reasons than this. Now think about the bar and restaurant areas. Why would it be important for them to know the rooms that people are in?

_____

_____

_____

_____

_____

You probably came up with fewer reasons than the housekeeping requirement, but it is equally important for the bar and restaurant to know where people are going, especially for requests such as wine in the room on arrival, or fruit selections in rooms etc.

You should always follow your own hotel's policy; my preferred method is allocation in advance as this makes check-in a lot smoother. If you allocate on arrival, then also print registration cards on arrival! My pet hate is handwriting on registration cards – you could be a 5 star celebrity hotspot, but as soon as you hand-write a room number on to the registration card it breaks the professionalism and looks tatty.

Allocation Crossover

On front of house, allocating in advance avoids the situation where you can see you have rooms available, but when going to allocate someone into a room there is no room that shows as vacant? Confusing isn't it? If you have rooms, why can you not put someone in a room that should be available?

This occurs due to 'allocation crossover'. To explain this look at the following table of a 3 room hotel; the names given are just example names of reservations that have already been allocated.

Room Plan 1

	01/01/2012	02/01/2012	03/01/2012
Double Room 1	Jones x 2	Jones x 2	
Double Room 2		Andrews x 2	
Double Room 3	Smith x 2		Martin x 2

Your system would show the following availability:

Availability 1

	01/01/2012	02/01/2012	03/01/2012
Double Rooms	1	1	2

So, we could in effect take a booking for a double room for 2 nights as we have the availability. But when it comes to allocating the room, we would have a problem.

If you look at room plan 1, you will see that there is no 'clear allocation' available so when we try to allocate a room for 2 nights, there is no space in any of the rooms for 2 nights in a row, only one night at a time.

The Guest Journey

What we need to do is move the allocated rooms around to make a room clear for 2 nights. What we do is re-allocate rooms, starting with the furthest possible date to do so, and this presents us with 2 options. We can either move 'Andrews' in to room 3, leaving room 2 clear for 3 nights, or move 'Smith' and 'Martin' to room 2, leaving room 3 clear for 2 nights.

The best solution is to move Andrews in to room 3, as with this one room move we have freed up one room for 3 nights.

So if we do that we have a room plan that looks like this:

Room Plan 2

	01/01/2012	02/01/2012	03/01/2012
Double Room 1	Jones x 2	Jones x 2	
Double Room 2			
Double Room 3	Smith x 2	Andrews x 2	Martin x 2

So now, we can out our new booking in to the available room to get a room plan like this:

Room Plan 3

	01/01/2012	02/01/2012	03/01/2012
Double Room 1	Jones x 2	Jones x 2	
Double Room 2	Johnson x 2	Johnson x 2	
Double Room 3	Smith x 2	Andrews x 2	Martin x 2

If a guest has specifically requested a room, this can cause problems. For example, if Andrews had specifically requested room 2, and Smith had specifically requested room 3, it would be almost impossible to take the Johnson booking... wouldn't it?

The Guest Journey

Not necessarily, remember that a request for a specific room is just that, a request! If you need to move the guest to another room to fit everyone in, then do it. Remember to try and ensure that you prioritise requests, so if a VIP requested a specific room, and a non-VIP also requested a specific room, you would opt to move the non-VIP first (where possible). Also ensure that everyone who is on the desk is aware that the request was made but could not be fulfilled! The receptionist on duty at the time of the guests' arrival should then explain that the request was made, but due to availability it could not be fulfilled and offer apologies.

Key Note:

There is an easy way to avoid this situation!

Remember: If someone is departing the room, someone should be arriving in to it! This will avoid allocation crossover situations!

So we have learnt how to avoid allocation crossover of a simple 3 bedded property, how about a larger property with 300 bedrooms? The same principle applies.

Can you see how allocating in advance has massive advantages? If you came across this situation when someone was checking in, it would take quite some time to resolve!

We have seen how allocation crossover can disrupt the allocation of rooms and cause a potential headache, but what about the actual allocating part?

How do you allocate rooms effectively?

You should always try to get rooms allocated 3 days before arrival, so during your 3 day pre-arrival checks. This is far enough in advance to troubleshoot any allocation crossover, yet close enough to take into account any out of order or out of service rooms (except for those last minute dramas!). It also is enough time for other teams to prepare and arrange staff should occupancy suddenly increase (e.g. when there is a local event on such as football).

Before beginning allocation, you should print a 'room plan' or 'room grid' that shows what rooms are already occupied on the dates you are allocating for. As a rule, you should print this from the date you are allocating for, through to 7 days after – this will allow you to see what is allocated for the full week.

Before actually allocating rooms in the reservation system, you should allocate rooms on paper, writing each guest name next to the room they will have on your rooming plan (most print in a similar format or layout to the room plan tables shown previously). By doing this, you can ensure your room allocation will be correct before committing it to the system.

When you have allocated on paper you should end up with a similar grid to the following allocation grid, which you can then transfer on to your live reservation system:

The Guest Journey

Allocation Grid 1

	01/01	02/01	03/01	04/01	05/01	06/01	07/01
01	Jones	Jones					
02	Martin						
03	Edward						
04	Cain	Cain					
05	Smith						
06	Ball						

When allocating rooms you should check which guests are VIP's and allocate them your larger and 'nicer' rooms; where possible you should also upgrade these guests (if policies within your hotel allow you to do so), and ensure this is commented on their reservation.

Always ensure that you have read the reservation comments and requests to ensure there are enough 'z-beds' or 'put-me-up beds'. Because you are allocating 3 days ahead, this gives ample time to contact housekeeping and arrange additional beds to be hired or borrowed.

If you come across an 'allocation crossover' you should resolve the issue there and then as failing to do so just means someone else has to, and they may not have the time to do it correctly!

The following list demonstrates the items you should look out for on reservations when allocating rooms, in the order you should check for them and allocate rooms:

1. **Room location** – if there is a function taking place that will be noisy, allocate the rooms above the function to guests attending the event. Allocate the function guests first in line with the below steps, then return

The Guest Journey

to step 2 when allocating all other guests, taking care to avoid putting non-event guests in to rooms above the function.

2. **Room type booked** – does the room you are allocating match the room booked? Remember to check the 'reservation changes' (if your system logs these) to see whether the room type was changed by someone to 'balance' the rooms.
3. **Additional beds or cots** – ensure the allocated room has large enough space to fit the bed or cot in to.
4. **VIP status** – should the guest have a larger room or an upgrade?
5. **Booking requests** – accommodate the booking requests where possible. For guests who have booked more than one room, or are part of a group, always allocate rooms close to each other.
6. **Everything else** – remember to allocate arrivals into departing rooms where possible

Once you have allocated rooms, you will need to ensure you hand over information to other departments. For example letting housekeeping know the amount of additional beds or cots needed; letting guest services or the concierge know about VIPs; letting the bar and restaurant know about requirements for food or drink in rooms.

As well as relaying all this information, you need to ensure that you take into account the configuration of your rooms. Many hotels operate on a 'zip and link' basis, where 2 single beds can be zipped together to create a super-king double, allowing the room to be used as a twin or double room. Because of this, it is imperative that you check at the 3-day stage, what room is required by the guest and pass this information to housekeeping.

This must be done if you use 'zip and link' rooms and is an extra factor to take into account when allocating (i.e. before doing step 5, you should look at what room configurations are already set up and allocate accordingly –

The Guest Journey

housekeeping will understandably be annoyed if they are asked to make 3 rooms in to twins, when 3 rooms are already set as twins but have now been requested to become doubles because allocations were done incorrectly).

Arrival Day

So, we have taken the reservation and then checked it several times to ensure everything has been routed, deposits charged and room types are correct, now we need to prepare our arrivals list for today.

The first thing to do is to print an arrival report for today that is as detailed as possible. If your system allows, you should print a report that gives you all the comments, payment information, rates, room types and other supplementary information such as VIP status.

Now you should double check the reservations to ensure everything is correct, including the allocated rooms, in the same manner as a pre-arrival check. Make any amendments as necessary as soon as you notice an error.

Printing registration cards

Once you are confident everything is correct, print the registration cards. Some hotels no longer use registration cards for guests and some print registration cards on arrival; each has its own advantages and disadvantages.

The main advantage of not having registration cards is that it consumes less paper, and means less for the guest to do at check-in. The disadvantage is that you cannot keep a full 'paper trail' of the guest information and have to solely rely on what has been inputted by the person taking the reservation or checking the guest in. Remember that not having the full details of the guest can breach several laws and regulations, depending on the country you are

Arrival Day

in, so always check the legal requirements for your hotel's guest registration policy.

For printing registration cards on arrival, the main advantage is that any last minute room changes do not result in having to re-print registration cards. The main disadvantage to this is that should your system fail, you would have no registration cards for guest to complete (unless you already have some pre-formatted and printed).

I prefer printing on the morning of arrival. This makes check-in a lot smoother as you do not have to wait for a printer to print the card, and also means that you have all the paperwork ready for when the guest arrives.

Once you have printed the registration card, you should either attach or file the appropriate reservation confirmation/backup. This should be somewhere that is easily accessible in the case of a dispute, but should also be secure and out of view of guests. If there are any deposit receipts that need to be provided to the guest, these should also be attached to the registration card, or filed alongside it so they can be presented to the guest on arrival.

Once we have the registration card printed with associated backup attached or filed, you need to ensure that any other departments that have special requirements are aware of what needs to be done (i.e. double checking there is a z-bed in the room).

If you have an ETA (Estimated Time of Arrival) for the guest, communicate this also to the relevant departments, such as the concierge or housekeeping, so that everything will be ready for the guest when they arrive.

It can be useful when there is a busy check-in expected (i.e. more than 50% of the rooms in the hotel are arriving) to pre-program key cards (if you use an

Arrival Day

electronic lock system) and attach these to the registration cards as it speeds up the check-in process.

> **Key Note:**
> If you print registration cards or allocate rooms on arrival, you should never pre-program keys for rooms. Also be very aware of your in-house electronic locking system cut-off times. Most are set to 12 midday after which time keys are usually reset so it is best to leave programming key cards until after midday,

Group Check-In

There are hundreds of variants of a 'group check-in' process and each has its merits. For large groups, such as coach parties, it is always recommended to pre-allocate rooms, and pre-cut keys. Usually the group check-in process will be one of the following:

- The entire group check-in one by one at the desk. Not recommended for units where there are less than 2 receptionists on duty and less than 2 terminals at the desk.

- The entire group is asked to collect their keys etc. from a table and are asked to fill in their registration cards and return them to reception. This is not recommended because several guests may fail to return their cards to reception, meaning you cannot be sure who is in-house.

- The entire group is welcomed (usually taken to a separate area of the hotel other than reception) and provided with envelopes containing everything to complete the registration process. The guest completes their registration card which they take to reception. This is the preferred method as the receptionist only needs to exchange the registration card for the key at the desk (after checking it has been filled out correctly of course!).

How you decide to do group check-ins is down to your individual hotel and what works best for you. Remember that if you fail to print registration cards for the group and just assume that everyone has arrived, you may be failing in your legal obligations, particularly if there is an emergency evacuation (you could be looking for a guest that isn't there!)

Arrival Day

Key Note:
Always look at whether a group check-in is necessary. If you have an in-house conference or event and people are staying as part of that, you can do a group check-in if everyone will be arriving at the same time. However if everyone will be arriving at different times, it would probably be better to do a single check-in process.

Use the space below to write down your group check-in process:

Arrival Day

Single Check-in

Even though this is titled 'single check-in' it actually applies to any set of arrivals that is for less than around 5 rooms, as usually these arrivals will come to the desk together and are expecting a slight delay in check-in.

There is one key phrase or question that should never be asked when a guest walks through the door - "Are you checking in?"

Let's be honest. If you turned up to a hotel laden with bags and walked to the reception desk, being asked if you were checking in would seem extremely pointless, and may even be the most obviously self-answered question you have ever heard! If you do this now... stop!

You would be surprised how revealing just a simple statement of 'good afternoon" (or morning or evening) will be. Just by making that statement to the guest invites them to respond and usually the guest responds with a mirrored statement, repeating your welcome, followed by what they are there for. So an example arrival is:

Receptionist: "Good Afternoon"
Guest: "Good afternoon, I have a room booked under the name of..."

If the guest does not respond revealing why they are here, simply ask "Can I just take your name?" This is a direct question which the guest feels compelled to respond to.

Usually they will say something like "The booking is under the name of..." or they may say "it's Bob Smith, I am here to see...." If they are here for an event or to meet someone.

Arrival Day

You can now begin the process of checking them in, so find their reservation on your system and double check with the guest to confirm the room type, length of stay and rate (e.g. "we have you booked in to a double room for 2 nights on a bed and breakfast basis"). This allows you to correct any errors before presenting the guest with the registration card.

Now complete your registration process (usually getting the registration card completed with at minimum the name, address, contact details and signature).

Key Note:
If the guest you are checking in is a foreign national (i.e. has visited from abroad for a holiday), you must ensure you get the details of their passport including issue date, passport number and where it was issued. This is also a great time to ask what time their return flight is and arrange for any late departure or early wake-up calls to be booked!

Most reception staff make a huge mistake at this point, and I am yet to come across a hotel where it has not happened! The crucial mistake is information overload, in other words telling the guest either what they know already, or telling them too much information.

Think about what you actually need to tell the guest. Look at the following list and decide which ones you think the guest needs to know on arrival:

Fire Evacuation procedures	Directions to the room
Where the bar is	Where the restaurant is
What time check-out is	Password for the Wi-Fi
Where the swimming pool is	How to contact reception
What your name is	How to request a newspaper
How to use the television	Room service times
Car park location and prices	How to ring a taxi

Arrival Day

How many did you circle? I personally would circle 5 of these for a guest who had never stayed, 2 for a guest who has stayed once or twice before, and just one for a regular guest.

Here is how I check someone in:

1. Greeting (good afternoon etc.)
2. Confirm reservation details and offer dinner or breakfast etc. if not included in package, offer room upgrade if available
3. Registration card completed by the guest during which I ask "Is this your first time staying with us?" (Unless they are a regular guest). Also ask if the guest wishes to leave a pre-authorisation of a card to allow extras to be charged to the room or take payment if not already done so by deposit.
    a. If it is their first stay then "Okay, well welcome to Pillow Inn, my name is Matt and I am the receptionist on duty this evening until 10.30, when the night manager will take over. As this is your first visit with us, could I just take a brief moment to familiarise you with the hotel"
    b. If they have stayed once or twice before then "Okay, well welcome back to Pillow Inn, my name is Matt and I am the receptionist on duty this evening until 10.30, when the night manager will take over" and skip to step 5
    c. If a regular guest, greet by name and skip to step 6.
4. Provide simple directions from reception to facilities (e.g. "Just through the lounge you will see the lifts, and to the left of these is the bar and restaurant which are signposted for you. All the opening times are displayed just outside the restaurant where you will also find the evening menu and details for breakfast service."
5. Provide simple directions to the room. NEVER state the room number to a guest who is alone, always point to the room number on their key

Arrival Day

    card and advise them that that is their room number. E.g. "You are going to be in bedroom xx which is located on the first floor of the hotel, just turn left as you exit the lift and you will see the room sign posted from there. "

6. Provide a finalisation "I hope you have a good stay, if you need anything just dial zero from your in room phone to contact reception."
7. Always offer to assist guests with luggage where possible (and you are able to do so), along with providing responses to any questions the guest may have.

You may have noticed that this seems like an awful lot of steps, but in fact, when you put them in to sequence and actually try it out, the whole process from arriving to getting the key takes about 2 minutes.

You will also notice that depending on how often the guest has stayed with us, dictates the amount of information they receive. If a guest stays several times, it can be annoying and sometimes insulting to be given all of the same instructions every time you check in. It would also be very frustrating to have stayed somewhere a few times but always be greeted like it is the first time you ever entered the building and that you know nothing about the hotel.

Arrival Day

Post Check-In

Once the guest has checked in, you will need to ensure that you update their details on your reservation system, ensuring you log any change of details to the address, contact details and make arrangements for any newspapers or wake-up calls. Depending on your procedures and set-up, you may also need to ensure details of car registrations and membership of reward schemes or leisure/golf clubs are also updated with the relevant departments.

Approximately 5 to 10 minutes after check in, it is strongly advised to call the guest in their room (or request your guest services team or concierge to do so), to check that everything is satisfactory and offer any drinks etc. to the room. This should always be done for guests who are staying with you for the first time. It demonstrates a pro-active, customer focused approach and ensures that any problems the guest has found are also rectified in advance of a complaint occurring. This is another opportunity to upsell any services or to even provide more information to the guest about the hotel or bedroom. Some hotels have procedures such as placing one set of towels in the top drawer of the chest of drawers; this would be the ideal time to inform the guest.

If the guest requested anything on arrival, such as a taxi booking or reservations for the restaurant, you should do these before ringing the guest as you can then confirm to the guest that this has been carried out. This also applies for wake-up calls and newspapers.

In short, use this call to confirm everything the guest has requested has been completed. Think about how long it takes for a guest to get to their room and get settled in; it probably takes around a minute or two to get to the room and a further couple of minutes to familiarise yourself with everything in

Arrival Day

the room so ringing around 5 minutes after they have left the desk is perfect for getting the guest at a fairly convenient time.

Do you think that you should tell a guest about any maintenance that is occurring in their room such as a bedside lamp not working, or a light switch not functioning correctly? Many would say no, but the correct response is yes! If something is not operating correctly in a room, you should advise the guest so that you do not get a complaint about it when they depart. Always apologise for the malfunctioning item and advise that your maintenance team have been made aware (ensure that they have!).

Now we have a settled in guest who is satisfied with their room and has had any courtesy arrangements taken care of. This is not the end of your journey with the guest as they will still interact with you throughout their stay. Think about how many times each day you see or speak to a guest, is it in the tens, hundreds or even thousands?

Chances are it will be fairly high, and possibly a lot higher than you may have originally realised. Now think about this figure and consider whether you included every time you email a guest, or simply pass them in the corridor? What about every time you answer the phone to a guest or give something to a guest? Each of these are interactions as well and must be handled correctly.

Arrival Day

Hotel with no life

I have seen reviews online and even stayed in hotels where guests describe the hotel as not having any 'life'; but what do they mean? A building cannot have life, nor can a building be changed without considerable expense, so how can you make it have 'life'?

The key to how vibrant a building is does not just lie in the décor; it also resides in the staff that are present. There is nothing worse than being treated like a room number or everyone 'sticking to procedure' all the time (this does not mean you can do whatever you like!). People are flexible and changeable, and you will need to be too. One certain experience springs to mind in a luxury 5 star hotel where I had cause to complain. When I asked to speak to someone to raise my concerns I was bluntly told 'well, you are not getting any money off your bill'. This is an example of not only incorrect complaint handling, but also the sort of response that engenders comments such as a hotel having no 'life'.

So what do people mean when they say that somewhere has no life? Do they mean it lacks atmosphere, or that it isn't loud enough? Possibly. What is generally meant by this comment is that the hotel lacked being personal to that guest. Regularly I tell staff to chat with guests, even if it is only to comment on something generally inane, such as the weather or a local event. You need to allow your own personality to come forward and for guests to feel welcome and at home.

Think about any time you have had someone staying at your house for a few days, or that you have stayed at someone else's house for a few days. Usually someone tells the visitor to 'make themselves at home' or similar? This is how it should be within hotels. Just like a guest in your home, a guest in a hotel wants to feel at home without 'treading on anyone's toes' (most of the

Arrival Day

time). They will make requests of you and ask you for information, but so would a guest in your home (such as getting a towel, or directions to somewhere nearby). So if you chat with guests in your home and talk about a variety of topics, why not with a guest in your hotel?

Write down a few 'conversation starters' in the spaces below; some short sentences or questions that could be used to get a guest engaging in conversation.

_____
_____
_____
_____
_____
_____
_____
_____
_____
_____
_____
_____
_____
_____
_____
_____
_____
_____

Engaging the guest

Try to think about the clientele that your hotel serves; this may be business people, leisure guests, families, weddings or any other assortment of reasons for staying. Now think about some topics of conversation for each of the guests your hotel serves. Here are a few tips:

Wedding Guests:

Asking the bride or groom if they are all prepared for the big day.
Asking family and friends if they are excited about the day (works particularly well with the bride and grooms parents and children)

Leisure guests:

Asking the reason for the stay – is it a short break away from the kids, or are they visiting local attractions or events?
Asking what they will be doing for the rest of the day (great opportunity to promote any in-house events or local events)

Business Guests:

Asking whether they are attending a conference locally or whether they are staying for work?
Enquiring what their business does (if you know the business name this is a great time to get some information about their business and get leads – perhaps they regularly use local hotels for business stays or use local areas for events?)

Airport Guests:

Everyone enjoys telling people about their holiday so ask whether they are flying out or just returning?

Engaging the guest

Where are they going / where have they been? (Perhaps you have been there and can recommend places to go, or perhaps you have always wanted to go there?)

Are they looking forward to going away / did they enjoy their holiday) – another great opportunity to provide exceptional service, perhaps you can arrange taxis or car parking for them?

Engaging the guest

Guidelines

There is always an opportunity to make a guest smile, or to engage them in conversation. Whilst it is recommended to enjoy yourself with guests, know where to draw the line by using the following rules:
1. NEVER say anything that could be deemed offensive, even if the guest states something themselves. This includes, but is not limited to:
    a. Swearing at or about a guest
    b. Making a derogatory statement regarding ethnicity, gender, sexuality, religion or nationality
    c. An expression of political, religious or other potentially offensive opinions that could cause offence
2. Do not fraternise with guests – this includes flirting, engaging in sexual or lurid behaviour and providing personal contact details for non-business related purposes.
3. Do not post images, comments or other material online that could be detrimental to your hotel, or your own professional image

These rules are important because you could easily cause massive offence to a guest, or anyone else who overhears the conversation; resulting in potential complaints, lost business and severe detriment to the reputation of your hotel – the easiest thing to do is remember that no matter how strongly opinionated you are, you should always remain neutral in all conversations, demonstrating no preference to any particular view. But how do you handle someone who is making potentially offensive remarks to you?

Dealing with offensive remarks

If they are making potentially offensive remarks about you personally, you are within your rights to ask the guest to stop. Something such as "I am finding your comments offensive. Please can I ask that you stop making comments such as those?" You can even ask someone else to take over dealing with the guest if you wish, just ensure you advise the guest that you are going to get someone else to help as you are unable to continue the conversation when they are making remarks that you find offensive.

Situations with guests being offensive are rare, but remember that you have as much right as the guest to be treated respectfully and with manners (although all receptionists know that guests do not always behave this way)! Have a think about what you would do in the following scenarios:

1. A guest talking to you refers to another guest in a homophobic or racist manner
2. A guest requests not to be served or dealt with by anyone who is non-British
3. A guest insults you personally in an offensive manner

What would you do in each scenario? How would you react? What would you say? The natural reaction would be to defend yourself or someone else, but here is what I would recommend for each scenario:

1. Simply refuse to comment. Explain that you do not hold the same view as them so would prefer not to discuss the issue or guest any further.
2. Advise the guest that there are many staff within your hotel from various cultures. Whilst they have made the request, it is not something that you would be able to uphold as this would be discriminating against certain staff within your hotel which would be detrimental and

Engaging the guest

offensive to other staff members. Remember that (particularly within the UK and Europe) there are laws and legislation which prevent discrimination of any kind based on ethnicity, religion, sexuality, gender and heritage. By conceding to the guests request you are likely to cause offence to those you work with and the hotel then may become liable for legal action by the employee; this is because the request would cause indirect discrimination against any employee who is non-British. By refusing the request, you are remaining within legislation; the guest may be unhappy but they will ultimately have to accept that the request is unreasonable and unlawful.

3. Advise the guest that your ability, ethnicity, or any other attribute they have attacked is not a subject for discussion and has no bearing on the matter at hand. You have the right to request the guest is dealt with by someone else, or ultimately, if there is no other staff member who can deal with the guest, or you are threatened, you are within your rights to request the guest be removed.

These are only suggested methods for dealing with the situations. You are not expected to tolerate personally offensive remarks, or to accept being discriminated against by a guest. Usually a polite request to refrain from making such remarks is enough to stop the guest from behaving in that manner. If ever you are assaulted by a guest, you should report the matter to your employer and the local police authority. Always operate a zero-tolerance policy on assault against staff or guests.

Now think about what you would do if a guest stated they were offended by someone staying in your hotel. I have dealt with this scenario several times and usually find that a quiet word with the guest causing offence is enough to elicit an apology and stop the behaviour. Ultimately you may decide to remove the guest from your hotel, and you should always confer with senior staff before taking this action. Only once in my years in hotels have I had a

Engaging the guest

guest removed from the hotel because they were being offensive to other guests; you have as much of a duty to protect other guests as you do to protect yourself and other employees.

Complaint Handling

Complainer Types

From time to time you will have to deal with complaints from guests. In a while I will cover some basic complaint handling techniques that can be very effective, but you will usually find that most guests will fall in to one of several types of complainer with differing danger levels (from 1 to 10, 10 being the most dangerous – the type of guest who could cause damage to the property and its reputation, and 1 being the least dangerous – the guest who will happily accept anything offered to them):

Silent Complainer
Danger level – 5

These guests are the ones who actually do not complain to the hotel. These are the guests who will never return again, but will not say anything to anyone unless pushed on the subject. These are the ones who usually provide negative feedback via comment cards or simply state that everything was okay – usually despite having had issues throughout their stay. The danger rating at 5 is because these are also the guests who will not tell you of any damage or issues in their room, or with service. This can be severely detrimental as there may be an unidentified issue that carries on for quite some time if you have several silent complainers having similar experiences one after the other.

Silent complainers can be identified usually in passing conversations where you overhear them discussing an issue with their partner or other guests. One particular giveaway is when an issue occurs and a passing comment such as 'here we go again' or 'typical!' is stated.

Complaint Handling

Dealing with these guests is tricky, mostly because you often do not know there is an issue. Silent complainers will usually transform into another complainer type when notifying you of their issues. If you identify a silent complainer because of a passing comment when something does happen, you should be pro-active. Apologise for the issue and ask for more information about any other concerns they have. Make the guest aware that you want to resolve any concerns they have as you want them to enjoy their stay.

Social Complainer
Danger level – 8

This is the guest who tells anyone who will listen about the issues that they have had. These guests rarely complain directly to the hotel, but will use social networking, online review sites and online media to berate their experience and the hotel.

Social complainers can be identified by comments such as 'this is going on TripAdvisor'. If the guest is in-house, they may well also make a review online whilst they are within the hotel.

Social Complainers should be dealt with carefully. Making an inappropriate comment or offer is likely to result in further complaint. You should always deal with these guests by finding out what they would like in order to resolve the situation and negotiating to a resolution of the complaint.

Complaint Handling

Empathetic Complainers
Danger level – 1

These are by far the easiest complainers to deal with. These are the guests who, despite having complaints, are very understanding and accepting of what you say. They are usually willing to accept almost any resolution that will be offered. These guests can usually be identified when they raise an issue and state that they 'don't want to make an issue of it, just wanting to let you know'.

These complainers are on the whole very forgiving and accepting of most situations. They can transform to social complainers if they are ignored or told that everything is fine. These complainers can generally be appeased with attentive listening to their concerns and assurances that action will be taken.

Offering an alternative room or small token such as a free upgrade on a future stay will usually be accepted.

Assertive Complainers
Danger Level – 7

These complainers are the type of guest who will be firm in their delivery of an issue and will usually have a preconceived idea of how they want the complaint resolved. They are usually identified by requests being made for certain things, such as requesting a free breakfast because of an issue, or a free room upgrade. These complainers will usually be fairly unwilling to negotiate and will have a determination to gain what they want.

Rated as danger level 7 because they can easily transform in to a professional, compensatory or aggressive complainer if not dealt with

Complaint Handling

appropriately. You may also find that this type of complainer will raise their issue to several different people if their demands are not met.

To deal with an assertive complainer, you should also be assertive. Start the complaint resolution by clearly stating your stance and what you can do for the guest. Offer alternatives to their request, or if denying a request, clearly define your reasons for doing so.

Aggressive Complainer
Danger level – 10

A very dangerous type of complainer because they become emotionally charged by a scenario, leading to irrational behaviour and aggression being directed towards staff. These are easily identified as they will vent their anger at a scenario towards however they are talking to. Physical and verbal aggression will always occur in the form of screaming and shouting, verbal abuse and personal offence at staff; property may be damaged and people may be assaulted (or assault may be attempted).

These complainers should be dealt with calmly and spoken to firmly and confidently (don't let them see the fear in your eyes!). Explain your stance on the situation clearly and offer an immediate resolution. Explain that aggressive behaviour is not tolerated towards staff (if necessary) and always avoid dealing with the guest alone. Try to get another member of staff present to assist in case of any personal assault attempt.

Direct the guest away from public areas and be attentive – nothing overcomes aggression better than someone who is being calm, polite and attentive.

Complaint Handling

Professional Complainer
Danger Level – 10

This type of complainer is very dangerous. They will not display physical or vocal aggression, but will be prepared for almost any argument or objection you may have. These complainers are the ones who are well informed (or at least believe they are) and have usually done some research before raising the complaint. These are usually not identified until post-departure, when you receive a written complaint outlining every issue that has happened, down to the smallest detail. The complaint will be backed up with references to legislation, generic standards or other material.

A professional complainer is very difficult to deal with, as they will usually leave you little room for manoeuvre in a complaint. Most of the time any arguments you have will have been pre-empted by the guest themselves and will be objected to in their complaint.

The most important thing to do with these guests is to be honest. Do not give obscure reasons, but be factual. Explain what has happened and what will now be done as a result. Address every cause for complaint in your response; leave nothing un-responded to, no matter how minor.

Compensatory Complainer
Danger level - 6

This is the sort of person who is 'in it to win it'. They complain because they want something out of their complaint, be it a refund, free future stays or upgrade. These types of complainer are rated as a 6 on the danger level because they generally will also show signs of a different type of complainer. Although they want something from their complaint, a consistently similar response from all staff will avoid any further action being taken.

Complaint Handling

When dealing with these types of complainer, they will often drop requests for items in to the conversation; e.g. "well, can we move to a better room", or "I will be happy if you…"

These types of complainers can be difficult to deal with as they may already have a pre-conceived idea of what they want to receive as 'compensation' for their complaint. You will usually find that you spend a lot of time during the conversation trying to convince them to accept a different resolution to the one they are requesting. Sometimes mistaken for an assertive complainer, but very closely linked as an assertive complainer will often become a compensatory complainer, or vice versa. The main difference between an assertive and compensatory complainer is that an assertive complainer will be fairly firm in their delivery and will be very fixed on what they want; a compensatory complainer is more commonly known as 'a whinger' and will often raise more issues throughout a conversation in order to magnify the effect of their complaint so they receive more in return. A compensatory complainer is usually more willing to negotiate and is less fixed on what they want to receive as 'compensation', they will be willing to accept alternate offers whereas an assertive complainer is unlikely to be truly satisfied unless they receive what they are requesting.

This covers some very common complainer types that you may come across, no doubt you can think of at least one guest that has complained to you that fits into at least one of the categories above. This is not an exhaustive list as everyone is different. Think of each complainer type as flexible; people and human nature is not static, it fluctuates according to each and every scenario the person is in. For example, the guest who stays and has an issue with a dirty towel may not say anything if they are there for one night before heading off on holiday for 2 weeks, thereby being an empathetic or silent complainer; but when they stay again for a wedding anniversary and find a dirty towel they may become an assertive, aggressive or professional

Complaint Handling

complainer. This is because their expectations of standards differ. For a one night break away, many things would be forgivable, but for special occasions, the guest will (understandably) be less forgiving over minor things.

Complaint Handling

The Three C's

So how do you handle that complaint? The trick is not in just identifying the type of complainer you are dealing with; that is just for knowing which 'hat' to put on when dealing with the issue. The main thing is to embody the 3 C's:

- **Confident**
- **Calm**
- **Collected**

Confident

People tend to have strange reactions to scenarios; I once managed a girl who burst out laughing when nervous or anxious, which did not serve well when dealing with aggressive guests. I have also worked with someone who could not handle any form of complaint through sheer terror at hearing the words 'I want to make a complaint'.

There is no trick or magic formula that will prepare you for complaints; I will sometimes be caught out by complaints from guests that have seemed perfectly amicable and friendly, but become aggressive or abusive as soon as there is an issue. As a receptionist, when dealing with complaints, your professional persona must not drop. No matter how friendly you may be with a guest, a complaint is still an issue that needs to be taken seriously. Never joke about the situation as this can only inflame the issue and cause a good relationship with the guest to break down.

Being confident is not about being aggressive, nor is it necessarily about being assertive (which is a common misconception); being confident is about having belief in what you are saying. The main thing to do is be honest with the guest. This is a common thread throughout complaint handling ('honesty is the best policy'!); deliberately misleading a guest will only lead to

Complaint Handling

further complaint, except the next complaint will be about you and will be much more difficult to handle!

So, to summarise, the key to confidence is being honest and believing what you are saying. If you lack confidence in complaint handling, spend some time listening to how other people handle complaints or even practice some role plays with a colleague.

Calm

Being calm is mainly about not getting angry or emotionally charged by a situation. Stick to the facts and do not pass blame for issues. Simply address everything in a calm manner – breath, breath again and then take all your rage out later on a beanbag!

Collected

If you are confident and calm, collected will come naturally. When you deal with a complaint ensure you have all the information you need or that you can get hold of it easily. Never let a guest think that you are unprepared or unable to deal with their issue!

Complaint Handling

Common Complaints

Here are some common complaints that are dealt with. Think about how you would handle these scenarios and what offers you would make to resolve them (we will talk about making offers later on, so keep a note of your responses).

1. A guest complains that their room is dirty. It is the first time they have stayed with you and they are very angry to find a mark on one of the bed sheets and a stain on the carpet.
2. A guest is unhappy with the food they had in the restaurant. The meal was fairly cold and bland. They accept the restaurant was busy and are 'just letting you know' as they check out. Their meal was included in their accommodation cost.
3. A guest arrives who has no booking in your system but has a confirmation email stating the room is booked via a third party travel agent. You have no rooms available to provide to the guest as you are fully booked and everyone has checked in.

Complaint Handling

Wants versus Needs

All guests have a set of certain requirement for their stay. These requirements and additional expectations are formed by the marketing of your hotel, previous stays at the hotel, previous stays at alternate hotels within your chain, online reviews, how their queries prior to arrival were dealt and many other factors. You will probably think that some of these are beyond your control, such as online reviews, but are they really outside of your influence? Online reviews are a big part of hotel choice for many guests and you have as much control as the guests.

Be very wary of guests that make a 'want' sound like a 'need'. There is a clearly definable difference between the two:

> **A want is something the guest would like to have. It is not a pre-requisite requirement, nor is it necessary.**

> **A need is something the guest must have and cannot be without.**

Something that is a 'need' for one guest, may just be a 'want' for another; for example a guest who is on a bed and breakfast rate needs to have breakfast provided as that is what they have booked; conversely a guest on a room only rate may want breakfast, however it is not a need unless it has been purchased by the guest. As another example, an able bodied guest may want a large room and may request this, however a wheelchair user would need a larger room in order to manoeuvre their wheelchair.

When dealing with complaints, you should always be aware of whether the guests request is a want or a need. This is because when it comes to making offers to the guest to appease the complaint, you should always try to meet their needs, and only offer wants as an added incentive. Think about the following situations and what is actually a need, and what is a want:

Complaint Handling

1. A guest has been placed in a double room when they requested a twin. It is 2 sisters sharing the room. They are unhappy at having a double bed as do not want to share, they require two separate rooms.

Now here you have a tricky one mainly because of the wording of the statement and how it is presented (another factor to be cautious of). The guest stated they requested a twin, which makes this a 'want' as they are unwilling to share a bed and they booked a double. This then becomes a 'need' as the guests need separate beds (it is something that is non-negotiable in the guest's view). The requirement for two separate rooms is a bit trickier. They have stated they 'need' two separate bedrooms, however only booked one room. You could give them two separate rooms, if you had availability, however that means one room is not being paid for (unless they agree to pay for an additional room). The 'need' for 2 separate rooms is actually a 'want'; the guest booked one room, presuming two single beds, therefore by providing one room with two single beds, you will be meeting their need; you would only be failing to meet their 'want'.

2. A guest states that they want a refund because of the noise levels in their room. They are being disturbed by other guests and are unhappy with the size of the room as it is too small.

With this issue, the guest has one 'need' – to find a quieter room. They 'want' a refund and also 'want' a larger room. This is a prime example of a complainer who has accumulated 2 issues in order to have more impact when they make their complaint – the issue of noise, and being unhappy with the size of the room. If you eliminate the noise factor, you are left with a minor issue of someone being unhappy with the size of the room. This may be because of a variety of things, but is generally not a cause for major complaint. If we address the 'need' of moving to a quieter room, regardless

Complaint Handling

of whether it is larger or not, the complaint will be resolved. Similarly you may wish to speak to the neighbouring guests to ask them to reduce the noise levels.

It can be difficult to gauge whether something is a want or a need instantly, and like a lot of things will take plenty of practice to get right. Before I talk about how to resolve complaints entirely, I want to cover some basic things to explain why people complain.

Complaint Handling

The Complaint Triangle

If ever you have heard of the 'fire triangle' (where you need fuel, oxygen and heat to sustain a fire – removing one element will dowse the flames), then this model will be easy to remember. There are 3 things that every complaint has:

Cause – Each complaint has a root cause

Emotion – The guest must be emotionally attached to the complaint (either through anger, despair or anxiety)

Desire – the guest must have a desire to complain and feel driven to complain about the issue

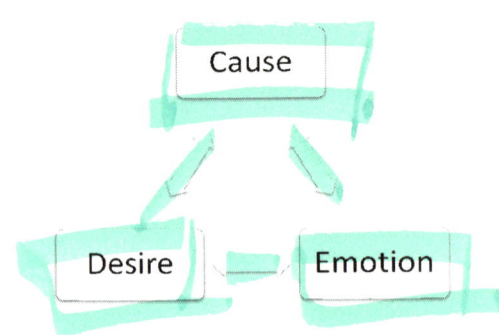

```
            Cause
           /     \
          /       \
       Desire --- Emotion
```

Eliminating one of these factors will usually cause the complaint to be un-sustained, just like with the fire triangle. To eliminate factors can be extremely simple when done correctly.

Let's look at eliminating the cause of a complaint. Many people will assume that this involves things such as restructuring rooms, having a full refurbishment or other grand schemes; whilst these things may reduce complaints they will not eliminate them as there are smaller things that often lead to complaints that usually get overlooked.

Cause

Complaint Handling

One way to eliminate the cause of complaints is to ensure you are aware of what people are complaining about. Some hotels keep a complaints log, which is best practice. You should ensure that you maintain data integrity, meaning you have a set of standard categories for complaints and place each complaint in to the specific category or subcategory (e.g. a master Housekeeping category with sub-categories of Room Cleanliness, Linen Standards, Bathroom Cleanliness etc. – create a category and relevant sub categories for each department such as Restaurant, Front of House etc.) This should be analysed regularly and management should monitor this log to ensure that specific areas of complaint are being targeted. Even minor issues should be logged (e.g. when issues are briefly mentioned as feedback or comments are left on feedback cards) as these can become major issues if not monitored. When an issue is resolved, you should also log how it was resolved. This then helps set a standard for resolutions that are offered and also provides information on the value of complaints.

Think about the following questions and whether your complaints log can answer them. If you do not have a complaints log, ensure from the start that you can answer these questions from the data it keeps:
- Can you tell how many complaints you had per department?
- Can you tell what the complaints in each department were about?
- Can you identify the most common causes for complaint?
- Can you see what was offered to each complainant?
- Can you see each complainants contact and hotel stay information?
- Can you see how much each complaint cost the hotel (i.e. lost revenue from free upgrades or free wine etc.)?
- Can you see how much complaints cost the hotel within a certain time period?
- Can you see how much each department or category of complaint type cost the hotel in free upgrades/meals etc in total?

Complaint Handling

Here is an example of the column titles for a basic complaint log on a spreadsheet:

Complaint date
Complainant name
Complainant address
Complainant contact number
Complainant email address
Complainants stay date (when they were in-house)
Department (complaint is about)
Category (type of complaint)
Comments (specific details of the complaint)
Employee dealing
Offer made
Value of offer (or nearest estimate)
Resolved (yes or no depending whether the guest has used the offer, for example a free stay)
Date resolved

You could expand this to include drop-down selections for offers and pre-format the values with lookup fields if you are an advanced user of spreadsheets, but you should at least have the fields above. More can be added as per your requirements if necessary; this should also be stored somewhere that everyone who will need to review or complete it will be able to access it.

Something else to consider with eliminating the cause is actually doing something about issues when you spot them. For example, I have seen hotels where a dirty cup is left in the foyer for the whole day; countless staff have walked passed it but done nothing with it. Take pride in your hotel and keep

Complaint Handling

it tidy. Remember that it usually takes a couple of seconds to be pro-active and get the issue resolved; it takes much longer to deal with a complaint! The same applies to issues in rooms – if you have no choice but to put someone in the room with a flickering light, then let them know that the issue exists and that you are aware, ensuring that your maintenance team is aware too!

Emotion

Now we have seen how to help with eliminating the cause we need to eliminate the emotion. Difficult? This is actually one of the simplest factors to eliminate and requires little work.

The main problem is that you can really only eliminate the emotion when actually dealing with the complaint and being reactive. The pro-active way would be to heighten the guests emotion on arrival. I do not mean by giving them kisses and cuddles or expressing your undying love for them (both of which are unprofessional and can be very offensive!), but by making the guest enjoy their check-in. I always chat to guests on arrival and talk about previous stays they may have had, where they are going to next or how the journey to the hotel has been. Just by taking an interest in the guest I am creating a temporary emotional connection, the guest is made to feel valued, welcomed and most of all, accepted! A common thread throughout life is that people want to feel accepted in to their surroundings and you are key to that in the hotel.

Some guests do not want to chat or have a conversation with me, which is fine; I will simply get them checked in and up to their room. Those guests who do have a chat and have a laugh on check-in will inevitably be the ones who are less inclined to complain, and when they do, will be much happier and willing to accept what I am saying; this is because, even though it is temporary, there has been a good level of rapport created (an emotional

Complaint Handling

bond based on mutual understanding) between us (just like being a guest in a friend's house, you would feel slightly uneasy telling them that their bathroom is dirty!). Again, you need to be pro-active for the emotion; a guest who likes you is less likely to get angry with you!

To eliminate emotion whilst dealing with a complaint you should simply be factual. Take notes whilst going through the complaint and use these to break down the complaint in to the key components. Once you have the key points of the complaint, reiterate these to the guest step by step to ensure you understand the key points of their complaint. Summarising the issues into a few sentences will also reduce the impact of the complaint in the guest's mind, making things seem less annoying than they first appeared. Be cautious when doing this to avoid being patronising. Repeat the details back to the guest clearly and in a neutral tone. Practice this with a friend or colleague and you will soon see how easy this technique actually is.

Desire

Let's now look at the final item – desire. A guest must be driven to make their complaint and must wish to have it acknowledged and resolved. This can be tricky to eliminate but it does tie in to emotion. Getting the guest to feel welcome and valued will often get minor issues overlooked by them. Each person has a set of emotional drivers that govern a standard model of thinking and reaction to situations; the following are the ones that drive many complaint scenarios:

- Control and Security – the desire to be in control of a given situation
- Recognition and Significance – the desire to be recognised and feel important
- Influence over others – the desire to dictate other people's decisions

Complaint Handling

Most people will present these quite freely when complaining, outlining their issues, what they want to gain and how they would like everything to be done. To overcome the desire of a complaint, you need to obey these emotional drivers. This does not mean giving in to the guest over everything; it merely means providing the guest with the fulfilment of these emotional drivers in at least one form. They do not have to be fully met; you can simply address and acknowledge each of them as follows:

- Control and Security – The guest will want to be in control of the situation and will want security over the matter also. This can be achieved by listening intently, and ensuring that you reaffirm with the guest that you will deal with the matters at hand. Create a personal connection by stating that you "will personally ensure everything is resolved and dealt with"
- Recognition and Significance – focus entirely on the guest and let them know you are taking the issue seriously, no matter how trivial it may seem.
- Influence over others – let the guest relay their issues and acknowledge each one. Let the guest know clearly that you are accepting everything they are saying and ensure that any offers you make are made on the basis of their complaint.

By recognising and acknowledging the emotional drivers that are behind the complaint, you will reduce the desire to complain, as the guest will be having their emotional drivers fulfilled.

Remember when I spoke about the 'fire triangle' where eliminating one thing will cause a fire to die out? A similar thing happens with this complaint model. If you remove emotion, the desire to complain is reduced (it can also be reduced if you heighten the emotion of a guest to a happier state). If you remove the desire by addressing emotional drivers, the emotional

Complaint Handling

involvement can be reduced. By removing the cause, you are guaranteed to remove the complaint as there will be nothing to actually complain about.

You probably think that the emotion and desire aspects are one and the same, but they are different. Emotion governs how we handle the situation and how we respond, whereas desire (despite being driven partially by emotion) causes the complaint to be notified. Desire can also stem from the guest having stayed previously and being disappointed with their stay and wanting to inform you of why they were less satisfied with this stay than the last; this is not necessarily emotionally driven, it may just be bare facts of a situation.

Standardisation

A closer look at the desire reveals some interesting aspects of the nature of a guest's complaint. Every person in the world has a pre-conceived idea of how everything should be. This is not necessarily based on the actual facts of a situation, nor is it based on the temperament of someone; it is based on their previous experiences. This is a process known as standardisation that everyone goes through during their life (it is a useful tool for training too!). Think about when you worked somewhere you hated or didn't enjoy working. You left and found a better job – why is it better? Is it better standards, better pay, brighter environment... all the above and more? You may be surprised to find that it often is not any of these specific things; it is because of your standardisation to your previous environment and role. If you spent 5 years in a windowless office, with one other person to talk to, then went to work in an open plan environment with many other people to talk to, you would probably instantly feel better about the role. This is because your standards of expectation were lowered by your previous role. As you spend more time in your new environment you will find that your expected standards increase, causing you to become accustomed to your surroundings. If you then went back to your previous surroundings, you would become de-motivated and unhappy very quickly. This is because your standard expectations were higher than those provided by your environment.

To summarise, standardisation is where your personal standards and expectations fluctuate according to your environment. The longer you spend in an environment, the higher (or lower) your standards will become, in line with your surroundings. The key here is that you have a set level of expectation, based on your own experiences, before even setting foot in an environment. This plays a key role in hotels.

Complaint Handling

Think about a guest who is staying with you for the first time. This is a guest who has spent the majority of their holidays camping or caravanning. They have never stayed in a hotel. Their standardisation level is low as they have no pre-conceived ideas of a hotel or what it will be like. Now say that the same guest stayed in your hotel, they would probably be 'wowed' by your service and rooms. However, your level of service and care has now become their standardised level as it has formed an idea of what hotels are like. The next hotel they go to will invariably be compared to your hotel. If that hotel provided a higher level of service, the guests' standardisation level would again increase. When they return to you, they have a higher standardisation level than they had the first time they stayed; if your standards are the same, they may be less satisfied as their experience does not match their standardised level.

The reverse also happens; a guest may be used to staying in world-class hotels with exceptional service and cleanliness. If that guest then stayed in a hotel with fewer facilities and lower levels of cleanliness, they would probably be massively disappointed. This is because their standardisation dictates that all hotels are the same high level of cleanliness and service. It would not be until they had either spent several days in a lower standard hotel that they would begin to overlook things. Returning again to a world-class hotel would (almost) instantly revert their standardisation levels for hotels. Standardisation may also occur due to other factors, such as the pricing of your hotel. Pricing at £10 a night means that people have much lower expectations of your hotel as they believe their stay will only have a value of £10. Now take the converse and say that a guest paid £100 for their stay. This may not seem much in business terms however it is a lot of money for many people. Having paid £100 for a room and then being placed in a dingy box-room would probably mean a complaint, regardless of how plush the rest of your hotel is. So to help with complaint avoidance, ensure that you allocate rooms according to the price paid. Work out who is paying more and who is staying

Complaint Handling

longer – allocate these guests in to the 'more luxurious' rooms and leave the smaller rooms either unoccupied or allocate them to the guests who have paid a much lower rate.

Transference

Have you ever heard the phrase 'In XYZ hotel we had...;? This occurs because you will always subconsciously draw a comparison between similar situations and circumstances; a process known as transference. To put this into context think about a bad experience you have had with a particular company or brand. How did the situation make you feel? If you went back to the same company, would you be expecting to have further issues with them? Chances are you would automatically assume a bad experience will occur; this is because you have had a bad experience with that company before and will subconsciously transfer that experience to the current situation, even though it may well be different staff or even a different location. The same thing happens in hotels; if a guest has had a poor stay with you previously they will probably expect a poor stay the next time they arrive. There is no way to avoid transference; it is a part of human nature. The best you can do is understand that when a guest refers to another hotel, or compares you to another hotel, or states that the service at XYZ was much better, do not take it as a personal slur. The guest is merely making a comparison to place into full context the complaint – transference allows you to make sense of a given situation; the comparison to another hotel is only created by the guest to enable them to fully comprehend and digest the situation.

Handling that complaint

There are many different quirks of human nature that dictate how someone will respond and behave in any given situation. This is determined by your stimuli throughout life and how you have been taught to react to situations by those around you. You do not know every step of every guest's life, so you should never try to presume what they will say or how they behave. Complaint handling is very much a reactive, rather than pro-active, process. This is because you have to react to the situation rather than just try to prevent it occurring. This does not mean that you should avoid being proactive and getting things fixed; it simply means that you cannot predict when a guest is going to complain, or what it will be about. I have worked in a hotel with bedrooms that had modifications for disabled access. Being pro-active and telling guests about the room modifications whilst checking them in is generally the best practice; however it was a very low percentage (probably less than 5%) of guests who were unaware on check-in, that actually complained about the rooms. This occurs due to a variety of factors; standardisation and transference are just two of them, but they are the main ones to consider.

Email/Written Complaints

Let's have a look at a complaint email and see what elements you can spot. See if you can identify the type of complainer; what issues they actually had; what standardisation had occurred previously; and any transference there may be.

Complaint Handling

> We arrived at your hotel with great expectations but that soon changed, your advertising does not convey that the hotel is actually positioned in a retail park. We arrived early to have a light lunch but were told that there was no food available as there was a private function on, we were directed to a restaurant across the car parks. When we returned we booked in and found that the room was very tired, there were stains on the furniture and mould in the bathroom. The bedside lights were both faulty but were quickly fixed after a call to reception. We found that the shower screen leaked across the floor and the rotten window, we had to place towels on the floor to soak up the leak. We booked for the evening meal and had a pre-dinner drink in the bar. We noticed the bar food menu and that we could have eaten here earlier instead of walking across the car parks. We paid extra to have choice off a better menu, the food was fine but the egg for the gammon never appeared, we mentioned to the staff and they gave a discount. Incidentally the next table ordered about 5 gammons, all arrived without eggs, had the kitchen run out of eggs? There was a very noticeable hum in the room which along with the outside floodlight above the window made for a very disturbed night. At breakfast there was a group of about 20 business people who started a loud introduction meeting at 08:30 in the restaurant, disturbing everybody else who just wanted a meal.
>
> We are not complaining people but overall we were just very disappointed, I realise we were using a voucher but we've had better cheaper. Last week we stayed at a fantastic hotel elsewhere and rated it as such on Trip Advisor, it's a shame we can't do the same for your hotel.

Firstly, let's figure out which type of complainer they are. The clue is all in the last few sentences; the guest has compared to a previous hotel elsewhere and has also mentioned an online reviews site suggesting they are a social complainer. Other details suggest they are a compensatory complainer (such as saying they are not normally the complaining type). Therefore we have 2 types of complainer crossing over.

Complaint Handling

Assessing the complaint

Let's look at the actual issues that the guest has:

1. Hotel advertising not clear on location
2. Being told there was no lunch available, then finding out there was lunch service
3. Issues within the room – faulty light, leaking shower, light outside, noticeable hum
4. Lack of food items
5. Disturbance at breakfast

So from a one page complaint, we effectively have 5 core issues that have instigated the complaint. Let's now look at the standardisation and transference they have – their standards are obviously higher than those they experienced, hence the complaint. But take a look towards the end of the letter; the guest states that they realise they were using a voucher but have had better cheaper. This indicates that the standardisation level they had prior to arrival was fairly low; however the marketing material raised the expectation of the guest. They have complained on several matters which indicates, despite them expecting the worst, that their standardisation level was fairly high. This is caused by the transference, referred to again at the end of the complaint with a comparison to another hotel in another part of the country. This is probably an unfair and unjustified comparison, however the customer has drawn the comparison on their mind (albeit subconsciously), which can make it difficult to pacify some guests, mainly because everything will be compared to something else.

Complaint Handling

Determining a response

So how would you respond to this? Would you instantly revert with an email denying everything, or would you respond to grovel and beg the guest for everlasting forgiveness? Or would you go for something a bit less extreme? No matter how tempting it may be to fire back a response to tell the guest exactly what you thought of them and how long it took to clean the room with all the blood sweat and tears that go into your working week and that receiving emails like this is soul destroying... don't send an email like that! You may be annoyed at receiving it, you should at least be down hearted by it as this is complaining about something you should have pride in – your hotel and service; but you should never become emotive in your response to a guest. Be factual and professional.

What you must do firstly is prepare your response. Think about what issues there are and weigh up your options. So let's look at our options (you may come up with more than these):

1. Give the guest their stay for free

This is not really a viable option. The guest has already stayed with you as the complaint has been received after they have departed.

2. Refund the guest for the stay

A lot of people would go for this option. It's easy and quick. However this can be really damaging – imagine if all your guests started finding out that they could get a free stay just by complaining. Not only that but the guest paid with a voucher so you can't really refund them for money they may not have spent themselves (it may have been a gift)

Complaint Handling

3. Give the guest a future stay for free

Again another commonly chosen option. Usually worded as an 'opportunity to show that we can get everything perfect' or similar. Another quick and easy option that does little to address many of the issues – what happens if the guest comes back and has a bad stay again next time?

4. Refund the extra they paid for the meal

The meal was a source of complaint, and it appears this was resolved at the time with a discount being provided. Making this offer would be a minimal gesture to the guest; the financial implication to the hotel is much less than refunding the whole stay

5. Give a future discount on a stay

Probably a preferred option and regularly overlooked. Offer the guest the opportunity to return on the same basis with a free upgrade of room or meal and wait on them hand and foot! Definitely preferable to the other options – the hotel will make money from the return stay, the guest has the chance to re-evaluate the service and there are no major financial implications. The guest stayed with a voucher indicating some form of special offer was used; therefore allow them to return on the same package with a free upgrade etc. This will also help you identify any compensatory complainer (as they will not want to return and will pressurise for a refund or similar).

6. Ignore the complaint

Never do this... ever.

Just don't.... Ever!

So we have determined (for this example) that we will offer option 5. Many people would happily start tapping away and writing the response now... STOP! You need to carefully think about what is going to go in to the

Complaint Handling

response and what action has to be taken. You should ensure the matters are notified to the relevant departments, and (where possible) each department should advise you of their comments or response to the complaint before making any offer to the guest (as they may suggest an offer that is different to yours). If this will take a couple of days, send the guest a brief email similar to the below:

Dear Mr Smith,

Thank you for your recent email regarding your stay at Pillow Inn. We take all guest feedback seriously and I am severely disappointed that you did not enjoy your stay with us.

I have passed your comments to the relevant team managers for investigation and would like to request that you allow 48 – 72 hours for us to look in to the issues raised so that we may respond appropriately.

Please be assured that I will contact you again once I have discussed everything with the relevant teams.

If you have any queries in the meantime, please feel free to contact me.
Kind Regards

This ensures the guest is aware we have received their email and are investigating. Never leave a complaint email more than 8 hours without some form of response, even if it is only an acknowledgement of the email being received.

Once we have received feedback from all the relevant teams regarding the issues we can look at responding to the guest in full.

Complaint Handling

So what do we put in our response? You need to think of the response in 3 key stages, the same as writing a story; it should have a beginning, middle and an end.

The beginning is very important. This will set the whole tone of the email response and should be opened professionally and factually. You should acknowledge the complaint and offer your initial apologies to the guest.

The middle should address each complaint issue and confirm to the guest what has happened as a result of their complaint. Each issue should be addressed in the same order as it was raised in the guest complaint. If a department passes on their apologies, offer them to the guest. Always ensure you have informed the guest of who has been informed and what action has been taken. Never over-exaggerate, if it was a one-off incident, say so! Never try to play down what the guest has said or try to 'make light' of the situation. Every complaint is serious.

The end is where you make your offer to the guest. You should ensure that you 'frame' the offer appropriately, do not just suddenly throw it in at the end. Finish with a 'Kind Regards' or similar (friendly but acceptable from a business perspective).

Complaint Handling

Sample Response

Dear Mr Smith,

Firstly may I offer my sincerest apologies for the issues you encountered during your stay with us. I have been in contact with all the relevant departments to ensure that the matters raised are corrected and would like to thank you for bringing these matters to our attention.

We are currently undertaking maintenance work on all our rooms in order to fix issues such as yours regarding the shower screen, along with redecoration and deep cleaning of all rooms within the hotel. I have passed your comments to the maintenance and housekeeping teams who will be undertaking restorative work before the end of the year to avoid future guests encountering such issues. Similarly, our maintenance team are carrying out inspections of all the air conditioning and generators within the hotel to establish, and hopefully eliminate, the cause of the hum you experienced in your room.

Our restaurant team would like me to pass on their apologies for the issues encountered with your meal, and our head chef is investigating why the gammon was not served as requested. Our restaurant and conferencing teams are also looking in to alternatives for large groups attending meetings, so as to avoid disturbance to other guests.

I would like again to offer our apologies for failing to provide you with the standard of stay you required and can assure you that your comments have been taken on board and are being acted upon so as to provide a much higher level of guest experience.

Complaint Handling

I trust this experience has not detracted from your opinion of the hotel overall and can assure you that the experience you encountered is not the typical experience we aim to provide for guests.

I hope that we will be able to welcome you back at some point in the future, and as a gesture of goodwill, I would like to invite you back to stay with us at a rate of £XX for Dinner, bed and Breakfast (the same basis as your previous stay), and I will personally arrange for your room to be upgraded to a premier suite and for your dinner to be served as private dining in your room without additional charge.

I hope you can accept this offer so that we may demonstrate our continued commitment to improvement and to show you the extremely high level of hospitality that we aim to provide at all times.

Thank you once again for taking the time to provide me with your feedback.

Kind Regards

You may have several interactions via email regarding the same complaint, and may have to adjust the tone of your letter to be firmer or softer dependant on the situation (i.e. do not tone a letter replying to a complaint about a stubbed toe with the same tone as one that is replying to a complaint from a guest who was burnt by hot fat being spilled over them!).

Complaint Handling

Face to face complaints

These tend to be a lot trickier to deal with as you do not have the luxury of being able to walk away and relax before responding and you cannot delete what you have said and rewrite it to sound better! You have to consciously make decisions there and then and immediately resolve everything when it is raised… or do you?

Many people think that the most important thing is to resolve a complaint quickly. Whilst I agree it is important to resolve the complaint quickly, it should most importantly be resolved correctly. Offering a quick resolution is nowhere near as valuable to a guest as being provided with the correct solution.

Here is a traditional scenario:
A guest approaches the reception and is unhappy about their room as it does not match the standard they expected and they are unhappy paying the amount that they have for the room.

Here is your crucial moment where you have to analyse and figure out what the complaint is about, what type of complainer the guest is, what you can do to resolve it, what the guest wants from the complaint, what the guest's name is, what room they are in, what they paid for the room and how long they are in the hotel for. So, first of all we remember our 3 C's – Calm, Collected, and Confident. Immediately acknowledge the issue and start to do something about it.

Complaint Handling

DEAL with it

Divert the guest to another area of the hotel, away from public areas.

Perhaps take them to a quiet area of the lounge or to the bar area if it is quiet. Make sure it is a quiet area and that there are limited opportunities for people to overhear you. Offer the guest refreshment such as a coffee or soft drink whilst you discuss the issue.

Empathise with their situation

Understand where the customer is coming from. £50 may not seem much to you, but to some people it will be a weeks' worth of food, or a month's worth of heating. Think about how you would feel exchanging the equivalent of a week's worth of food to be put in to a setting that is far lower than the experience you expected.

Ask the guest to explain all the issues they have

Get the guest to explain everything in their own words, exactly how they see it.

Listen intently

This is fairly obvious. Never offer a resolution without actually asking the guest what the issue is in the first place.

Complaint Handling

The magic question

Okay, remember that I have said before that there is no magic wand to resolve or fix things? Well there is one piece of magic I believe in and it all lies in a simple question that can either let you know exactly what the guest wants, or it will allow you to make almost any offer and for it to be accepted. What are these words I hear you cry? Very simply:

"How would you like me to resolve this issue for you?"

That's it. Some people use this already or a variation thereof and some use it incorrectly. Some have heard of it and some have never even seen it on the horizon!

The reason this works so effectively is because either way, you are winning from the situation. You will either know exactly where the guest stands or you will have the freedom to offer as much, or as little as you deem necessary. Think about how you would react if you had a complaint and you were asked this question after you had explained everything to the person dealing with your complaint. You would usually do one of three things:

1. Be a bit stunned and not really know what to say as the question took you by surprise
2. Explain exactly what you want to resolve the issue
3. Pass the question back and ask what the person is going to do to resolve the issue for you

Option 1 is fairly easy to deal with. You can assess everything and make an offer based on what suits you and your hotel at that time.

Complaint Handling

Option 2 is also easy to deal with, you have hit the point of honesty and can spell out exactly what you can and can't do.

Option 3 is the trickiest as you have had the question reversed towards you. A simple response of 'I am trying to work out what the best solution is for both of us and just wondered if there was anything in particular that you feel would resolve the situation in your mind?'

So we now have reached the tipping point of the conversation. When the guest approached the desk to complain, they held full focus of the conversation and had full control of the situation. Now they are engaged in conversation and have exhausted their initial purpose of telling someone they have a problem. Now the control of the situation reverts almost entirely to you (although you inadvertently have been in control the whole time by deciding where to have the conversation and who is going to deal with it). The guest will be waiting for you to respond to their issue and offer a solution. If you want to reach tipping point quickly, just ask the 'magic question' and it will be reached within a few seconds! Now you will need to think about your response.

Complaint Handling

Responding face to face

Repeat

Paraphrase the issues back to the guest, explaining your understanding of each one and the impact this has had on the guest (e.g. "You found a broken tile in the bathroom which is a concern to you as you have a small child and she could cut herself").

State your position

Make the offer by firstly stating what you can and cannot do. If you are full, explain this to the guest but offer an alternative solution. Believe it or not, there is always some form of solution to a crisis! I will not spoon-feed you solutions to problems as you will need to come up with ones that suit your needs and hotel!

Gain understanding

Ensure the guest understands your offer and the reasons for this. For example, a guest who discovers a broken bathroom tile could be moved to a vacant room that has not yet had a guest check in to it. The room could then be cleaned and temporarily fixed for the next arriving guest (even if it is masking tape over the tile) – as long as the arriving guest is aware on check in, or the room could be put out of order if you have the availability to do so!

Follow up

Ensure you make a point of seeing the guest later that day or the following day to ensure they are satisfied with the outcome of their issue.

Complaint Handling

A lot of the time, people are offered free upgrades or a few drinks at the bar to resolve an issue, and most of the time this is totally unnecessary – all guests have basic requirements:

Provide what I expect and get everything right the first time!

Points to take on board with complaint resolution offers

Room moves can be very inconvenient guests. Most guests would prefer to have something fixed rather than having to move rooms as it is an inconvenience to have to drag your luggage across the hotel and re-pack everything!

A free drink will not repair the broken television or make the room warmer, nor will they help a guest forget the way they have been spoken to by a member of staff.

If you screw up, you fix it! Do not expect other people to continuously cover up for you. If you put the guest in the noisy room when they requested a quiet room, admit it and apologise to the guest – believe me it is appreciated a lot more when someone admits they have made a mistake and comes forward to help resolve it. This is a mantra of mine throughout my management career; believe me when I say that you learn from this very quickly and the guest is much happier with the resolution.

A refund will not make everything perfect! Reimburse room costs at your peril – the guest's level of standardisation will not suddenly fall a lot lower because you cut the price of their room. The guest may seem happy but in reality, has the core issue actually been resolved?

Ensure that other teams are aware of the complaint and what the outcome was. Email them or leave a note in their pigeon-holes to let them know; just make sure they are informed. You may from time to time want to get them involved in the complaint handling process (e.g. if a guest complains about food service, it would be worthwhile ensuring the restaurant manager is part of the conversation and resolution). It is also not rude to advise a guest that

Points to take on board with complaint resolution offers

you will look into an issue and come back to them later in the day. Define a time that you will have a response for the guest and ensure they know where to come to speak to you. If you do not speak to them, write them a short letter outlining the action you have taken and leave it in their room for them, with one copy of the letter left with the receptionist on duty so they are aware of what needs to be done (if anything).

There are many different sources of information out there surrounding complaint handling and I would recommend further reading and practice on this particular subject if you deal with complaints regularly. What you must do is ensure that you resolve the issue, no matter how long it takes. Many receptionists will refer complaints to management, which is acceptable in most cases. Be aware that reception staff should be enabled to resolve complaints and deal with minor issues without management involvement.

Overbookings

It seemed natural to talk about overbooking of the hotel directly after complaint handling. I personally am against overbooking of hotels; I was once told that not overbooking was commercial suicide, and many people also share this point of view. I will not force my opinion on to you however be aware that whilst you may disagree with overbooking, if your hotel runs this policy you will have to abide by it.

Overbooking is a gamble. It is the process of allowing more rooms to be sold than the hotel physically possesses, in the hope that some of the guests will not arrive or will cancel at the last minute. In some cases you will have people who don't turn up, in some you will have everyone turn up, in some you will have last minute cancellations; in every circumstance reception will be involved at some point.

If you work on reception and also deal with reservations as part of your role, you will be aware of overbooking far in advance of the actual date you are overbooked for. At minimum you should be aware of your availability for the next 3 days so you can deal with any last minute enquiries from guests wanting to extend their stay, or any walk-ins you may have. It also means that you can begin to prepare for any out-booking scenarios.

On a daily basis, you should call around local hotels and check availability for their rooms. This is not just to be prepared in case you become overbooked, but it is also to assess local business – there may be hotels that are overbooked that you can sell rooms to. When ringing hotels you should always adhere to the following guidelines:

Overbookings

- If you are overbooked always ring the hotels that are closest to you both in terms of location but also in standard and facilities. Basically, do not out-book a guest from an executive penthouse suite to a backpacker's hostel or similar!
- If the hotel you are ringing is overbooked, offer them rooms at your hotel if you have availability and offer to negotiate on the rate.
- If the hotel you are ringing has rooms and you need rooms that evening, always try to negotiate on rate and, where possible, try to get the rates matched so the room does not cost more than the guest is paying.

Causes of overbooking

Being overbooked indicates one of three things – either your hotel has high demand, or the area has high demand. If it is your hotel that has high demand, out-booking is fairly easy (but has its pitfalls as you will see in a moment); if the area has high demand, it is a lot more difficult to out-book as other hotels will also be full. The third thing is just poor sales management – I won't cover this because the solution is simple – stop selling when your hotel is full!

High demand for your hotel

Overbooking can be caused just simply by high demand for your hotel. This will be caused by several things, the most common being exceptional demand for your service through reputation or through exceptional offers. You will have little control over rate management on reception, but if you do have control of this, be aware of local events and vary rates in line with your competitors – do not cheapen your hotel by selling at a ridiculously low rate just for the sake of getting people in to the hotel!

High demand in the local area

This occurs when you have local events, such as nearby football matches or concerts etc. It is more difficult during these periods to arrange out-booking of guests, mainly owing to occupancy levels and availability of nearby hotels. Similarly the cost of out-booking increases because as demand increases, so do prices.

Overbookings

How to out-book

You can do one of two things when out-booking, either pro-actively out-book guests, or gamble on arrivals. I will not try to influence your decision as it is whatever works best for you. Discuss the options with your management team as each has their own advantages, depending on the situation and local availability.

General out-booking.

Firstly you need to select the guests that would be most suited to out-booking. This can depend on a number of factors; generally you should choose only leisure guests (not any linked to in-house events, corporate bookings or travel agencies) for out-booking. This is because it minimises the risk of losing any big business contracts and also means any complaint is retained within the business. Once you have narrowed the selection down you will need to find out where there is availability in the area and what rates you are able to get rooms for. Sometimes hotels in the area will rate match for you, meaning the guest is not charged anything more for their stay; if the hotel will not rate match and is more expensive, you should be aware that any difference in cost should be picked up by your hotel, not passed on to the guest. If the other hotel is cheaper, the saving should be passed on to the guest as a compensatory gesture.

Proactive Out-Booking

Being proactive about overbooking means contacting the guest prior to arrival; and informing them that due to unforeseen circumstances you do not have a room available for them for the evening but have made alternative arrangements at another hotel; provide the guest with full details of the alternate hotel that has been arranged including website address, street

Overbookings

address and contact details. This has the advantage of balancing your room occupancy prior to the overbooked date. The risk is that you could end up with empty rooms if you have any last minute cancellations or non-arrivals. It does however guarantee that you will not have to deal with out-booking guests at the last minute and also means that guests can go directly to the alternate hotel, without having to travel to you first. When being proactive with out-booking, always waive any cancellation policies; if you are refusing to accommodate the guest, the least you can do is allow them to cancel free of charge!

Reactive Out-Booking

This is when you out-book people as they arrive. The out-booking is done on a last-in, first-out basis. For this form of out-booking you will need to ensure that no rooms are allocated as they will have to be allocated as people arrive. Once all rooms are occupied, any arriving guests are then out-booked to nearby hotels. This has many risks. You may end up out-booking a very important client; local hotels may not have availability; you may have to pay last minute booking rates leading to a major loss on the cost of a room. Surprisingly, this is one of the most commonly used forms of out-booking; this is because the hotel is hoping that people will not turn up or will cancel last minute leading to less requirement to out-book.

As a receptionist you will need to deal with the guest face to face when they arrive and they will probably not be too happy about the situation. You will need to explain that you have no availability due to an oversight by the hotel on availability. Provide details of their alternative accommodation and explain some of the benefits, such as enhanced facilities or an upgraded room at the same price etc. Refer the guest to management to handle as a complaint if the guest remains dis-satisfied.

General Guidelines

Whichever method you choose to use for out-booking, you should be aware of the risks and advantages of both.

Proactive Risks	Proactive Advantages
You are guaranteeing some rooms to be booked out. This guarantees unhappy guests and also sets a fixed cost to the hotel for out-booking the guests. If the guest does not arrive to the other hotel, you will probably have to pick up the cost.	You know how much the hotel is going to lose in advance. Receptionists do not have to deal with guests complaining on arrival. The guest is more well-informed and can decide whether to stay or cancel their room in advance
Reactive Risks	**Reactive Advantages**
You could annoy a very important client and/or lose business. Your reception team will have to deal with complaints. No rooms are held so there is no guarantee of finding a room quickly nearby.	Everyone may not show up, meaning less cost due to out-booking.

Overbooking is a risky business with advantages and disadvantages to almost every scenario. You should always carefully check all your bookings before out-booking to ensure there are no errors or duplicate bookings that could cause further issues. Here are some general rules for overbooking:

- Maintain your availability correctly. Do not allow your hotel to become overbooked by ridiculous amounts. 5 or so rooms are a general maximum for most hotels – a general guideline is not to be overbooked by more than 10% of your total occupancy (so if you have 50 rooms, overbook by a maximum of 5)

Overbookings

- Don't Panic. Overbooking happens. The main thing to do is remain calm. You can only deal with the situation as best as you can. Try to get as much as possible prepared.
- Watch out for groups. Never split a booking of several rooms so that some are staying and some are out-booked, always either keep them all in-house or out-book them all.
- Only out-book for the nights you need to. If you are overbooked for only 1 night, you will have guests who are in-house for only one night. These are the preferred ones to out-book. Avoid having a guest stay somewhere else for one night then with your hotel for one night; this is more stress and upheaval than the guest deserves.
- Limit your costs. Do not out-book to the 5-star hotel up the road and expect them to only charge £20 more than you! Avoid over-spending on out-booking costs; many guests are more than happy with an equivalent room and hotel to that originally booked.

Cash handling

Most hotels operate a standard cash handling policy that should be adhered to at all times. This policy usually covers actions to be taken in the instance of monetary discrepancies in floats or shift cash drops as well as control of access to money within the safe and tills at the front desk.

As a bare minimum you should always adhere to the following:
- You are responsible for all the money that is within your immediate control. This includes ensuring the credit card machine balances with your shift takings, that all floats balance at the beginning and end of your shift and that any monetary withdrawals from the safe and deposits to the safe (i.e. petty cash, receipt of change orders etc.) are balanced and correct.
- You should always ensure that you do not relinquish control to someone else for money that you are responsible for. It may feel uncomfortable, but even if your manager requests money from the safe the amount should be counted, verified and countersigned by you as correct.
- Ensure any cash is kept locked in a secure place away from guest view. Most hotels have a drawer, till or cash tin that is locked when not in use. Do not allow anyone else access to your cash floats without being present yourself to verify their actions.
- Never exchange cash for a cheque or credit card transaction (unless permitted by your hotel). These can hold serious financial implications as cheques may bounce and the credit card may have a transaction fee that means you may have given out more in cash than the hotel actually received from the card payment.

Cash handling

- Count every penny in and out of your floats and safes. This includes any deliveries of change – count it all to make sure it is correct before signing to accept delivery.
- Anyone who takes money out (e.g. for petty cash purchases) should be made to sign a receipt for the amount (usually known as a petty cash voucher); this should then be included in your float checks as partial balance towards your float.
- Never let anyone else process payments or transactions using your ID or login for any systems. If they wish to process a payment they should do so on their own ID or they should ask you to complete the transaction for them.

It is recommended to review your own cash handling policy from time to time, even if only as a refresher.

Shift Checklists

Most hotels operate with a three-shift reception system consisting of a night shift, morning or early shift and afternoon or late shift. Usually these operate at times of around 7am to 3pm for early shifts, 3pm to 11pm for late shifts and 11pm to 7am for night shifts; each hotel varies however the hours are usually similar to these across the industry. Sometimes there will be a mid-shift of around 10am to 6pm or similar, in order to assist with a busy departure or arrival schedule. Regardless of the shift you are on, the hotel will commonly operate a shift checklist to ensure that a number of common tasks are completed on a daily basis. Sometimes these will be arranged so that certain tasks fall on certain days (such as checking an order for more change for the restaurant or bar has been placed on a specific day).

It is important to know that shift checklists are not just there to ensure things get done as they are also there to help your fellow team members. Imagine if you forgot to check everyone out of the system and the late shift had to spend time checking people out just so they could get on with their roles. It would get very frustrating if this was continuously happening.

Shift checklists should be there as a guide to let you know the most important things to be completed on a day to day basis and are also an effective management tool. I have spent many months perfecting shift checklists in the past, amending and altering them upon reviewing the tasks that people undertake. If you think something is not on your shift checklist but should be, then let your manager know. If you do not run shift checklists, speak to a manager about getting them instigated.

It is important to note that not everywhere is suitable for shift checklists. Some larger hotels operate reception desks where checklists are not feasible or

Shift Checklists

where the main duties of reception are to meet and greet and get people checked in. For smaller hotels this may not be feasible, so a shift checklist becomes extremely useful as it ensures that the administration work is completed for the following shifts and that everything is correct prior to the receptionist leaving for the day.

I could put here a sample checklist, but it would do little to actually help as each checklist varies according to each hotel and all the tasks that are required for each shift within that hotel. Some example tasks include:

- Log in using your ID (surprisingly a lot of people forget to do this!)
- Count and reconcile all floats/safes
- Complete 1, 3, 7 day checks
- Check all guests in/out
- Bank out and balance all financial reports

Keys

One of the core responsibilities of any reception is to control access to areas of the hotel. This usually means that you will have full responsibility for managing who has what keys and when.

Most hotels have a key log, where people sign keys in and out when they are taking or returning them and this should be enforced by reception at all times. This is so you can easily track down where keys have gone if they go missing and so that everyone knows exactly who has the keys at any given time.

If you use an electronic key system you should always ensure the following:
- Keys are programmed for the appropriate number of days for the guests stay; nothing is worse than having to go to reception to get the key reprogrammed every day
- Only de-program a key if you are permitted to do so (see 'lock-outs')
- Do not leave master keys or lock programming passwords within guest view or reach.

Lock-outs

This is where you de-program a key to prevent access to a specific area for a guest or group. This can occur for many reasons;

- Accidental lock-out. This happens when a guest has left a room and the key is still within the room. In this instance the duty manager or maintenance will usually be able to allow access back in to the room for the guest.
- Time-sensitive lock-out. This happens with electronic locking systems from time to time. Usually most rooms will have a standard cut-off time (for example a key programmed for a bedroom tonight will expire at midday tomorrow). If the guest has a late departure of say 2pm, their key will not operate beyond midday and will need reprogramming.
- Purposeful lock-out. This happens usually when it is required for a guest to attend the desk for one reason or another. Commonly this is used by hotels for guests that have an outstanding or high balance that needs to be cleared prior to any further stay being allowed. It may also be used to arrange for guests to move rooms or provide witness statements for incidents etc. Never use this just to deliver a message to the guest or just 'for a chat'!

Messages

Guest messages are important. You should always try to ask the person leaving the message how urgent the message is. You do not want to interrupt a very important meeting for a phone call from a partner asking them to pick up some milk on the way home; but you also do not want to delay the news that a relative has been taken seriously ill.

You will have to use your discretion as a receptionist to determine whether or not you should get the guest now, or whether it can wait; usually the caller or person leaving the message can let you know this. For guests who are in their bedrooms, you can usually transfer the call directly. For guests at conferences or in-house events you may need assistance from other staff to get the message delivered to the guest.

Urgent or distressing messages

If the caller states the call is urgent immediately contact a manager, porter or other staff member to attend the guest's room or conference and personally retrieve the guest so they can take the call. Offer a private space to take the call (even if this is in the back office or in an empty bedroom) and leave them alone to take the call; do not hover over the guest whilst they are on the phone. If the guest is distressed or upset, immediately offer a private area for them to stay in whilst they gather themselves, along with complimentary use of a telephone or internet facility.

If the news is particularly distressing, offer a refreshment and use of the facilities; offer to contact any family members and arrange any transportation or taxis that may be required. Act with the guest in the same as you would a friend. Do not offer cuddles and hugs, but allow the guest to

Messages

have privacy and relieve some strain by making any necessary travel arrangements for them (such as ringing the airport to rearrange a flight, or booking a taxi). Under no circumstances offer the guest an alcoholic drink if they are to be driving!

Non urgent messages

Other messages that are non-urgent can be placed into the guests pigeon hole, slipped under their door, placed in their room or added to their in-room television system (if the guest has a bedroom), or they can be delivered to the guest during a break from the event. Never leave them on the side and forget about them.

Delivering messages
When delivering a message is should be written verbatim (word for word as spoken to you) onto a piece of headed paper (or preferably typed up and printed) and placed in a sealed envelope with the guest's name on the front. Never disclose the contents of a message for a guest to anyone except the guest themselves.

Events

Most hotels hold some form of event from time to time, be it a private dining event, wedding, conference or office party. How each is handled is crucial to the success of the event. Here are some guidelines for dealing with some common scenarios:

Any event:

- Know where it is taking place and how to get there, this is so you can direct guests appropriately.
- Know the time everything begins and what guests are to do prior to the event starting – do not allow guests to accumulate in public areas unless already agreed with the event organisers. Similarly, do not send them to the event area until you have been advised it is acceptable to do so.
- Know who the main organisers are and when they will be arriving. Nothing is worse than attending an event that you are organising and for no-one to be ready for you.

Conferences and Seminars:

- Usually these are charged per delegate, so ensure you have enough registration forms printed for guests to sign in to the event.
- Ensure you know the variations of each conference event's name. There may be many different people from many different companies arriving and all may know different variations of the conference name. Knowing as many of the possible variations as you can speed up the registration process.

Events

Weddings and Parties

Know who is in which room in the hotel. Ensure that the party guests are allocated into the bedrooms above where the party is taking place as they will be less likely to be disturbed by, or complain about, the noise from the celebrations. Also know where the organisers or bride/groom are staying.

Guest confidentiality

This is very unusual to be included in a training manual about reception, but it is one of the informal rules of reception.

No-one exists.

Sound strange? It really is fairly simple; if someone asks for details of where a guest is staying, you should refuse to provide the room number unless they have a legitimate reason for knowing, and even then you should be cautious.

The best policy is to politely refuse to provide room numbers to anyone who asks (unless of course they have lost their key and cannot remember their room number in which case you should verify the name, address and any other information you feel necessary to feel confident they are the person staying in that room). Advise the person requesting the information that for the security of all guests you are unable to release room numbers to guest. The person at the desk may however be allowed to use the reception phone to call the guest and find out which room they are in (obviously with you dialling the room number so they cannot see it).

If you are suspicious about the caller or person wanting a guest's room number, ask them to take a seat whilst you have a look at the records for them (usually the ploy of the system having problems and going to check the manual records will work well). Go to the rear office of reception (ensuring you have locked access to your terminal at the front desk) and discretely call the guest in the room and enquire if they wish their details to be released and then act upon their instructions. If they do not want details released, advise the enquiring person that there are no records of any guest under that name within the hotel.

Guest confidentiality

Many hotels will operate an incognito service, whereby the guest's name on the system is altered to that of an alias or pseudonym so the guest may not be located easily. This is commonly employed by celebrities and high-level public figures. This should always be adhered to and many systems have a facility in place to allow a guest to be incognito.

Marketing Materials

Although you have little control over marketing from within reception, you still have a responsibility to ensure everything is up to date. Under no circumstances should you allow out of date materials to remain on display. It is extremely poor service having to explain to a guest that the brilliant offer they just saw on a poster in reception actually ran out a week ago!

Utilise the materials you have available. If you have feedback cards, prompt guests to complete them. If you have business cards, give them to guests who are enquiring about staying in the future.

Departures

Okay, so the guest has stayed and had a wonderful time with you and now comes the time to depart the hotel. It is important to be alert for guests approaching the desk to depart the hotel – usually you will hear them approaching as they come down the corridor or through the lobby. Immediately you should stand to greet them before they reach the desk and should also ensure you have your departures screen loaded ready to check them out.

When the guest reaches the desk, greet them with a friendly 'Good Morning' and ask them for their room number (although the best receptionists will know this already as they will recognise the guest!).

If the guest has a balance to pay you should print a copy of their invoice and ask them to check through the invoice before requesting payment. If the guest is satisfied with the bill, process their payment. Any invoice queries should be resolved quickly and any necessary corrections made (such as a guest being charged for 2 breakfasts when they only had 1) – serious discrepancies should be investigated with the assistance of a manager.

At the point of departure you should always enquire whether the guest has enjoyed their stay. This is also a perfect opportunity to have any comment cards completed by the guest. If the guest has had any issues, make a note of them and pass these to a manager, advising the guest that you will get them looked in to and thanking them for letting you know.

If the guest had issues and complained during their stay, instead of asking if they enjoyed their stay, ask if everything was resolved to their satisfaction and offer your apologies again for the issues they experienced.

Departures

Once the guest has settled their account and checked out, offer assistance with on-going travel arrangements such as taxi's, train times or directions. Offer assistance with luggage or the use of an umbrella if it's raining – do not let the service slip just because the guest is leaving – the service should never stop – after all the guest may ring up later that day to book a room for a few months' time.

That's all folks… sort of

There will no doubt be future revisions of this book and future additions. This was always designed for medium sized hotels and never as a one-size fits all solution so you may have to vary some of this information to suit your own needs. I know a lot of this may seem daunting, but if you take on board most of what is in here, and combine it with other training and on-the-job learning and experiences, you will quickly excel as a receptionist! You will notice there are some things I did not talk about, such as dress code – to be fair if I have to tell you how to dress to make a good impression, then find a different career. I hope you have enjoyed it, I found it hard to stop writing, so please excuse any ramblings – I hope that even if you only took a few snippets of help, that they were worthwhile!

Emergency Measures:

This is my final bit of this book and is a simple guide to what to do in some emergency situations that may occur:

Guest arrives with booking confirmation from a travel agent, but no booking in your system:

- If you have a bedroom, get them booked in to it. Offer the guest a seat whilst you arrange their registration card.
- If you have no bedrooms, invite the guest to take a seat whilst you investigate their booking as there appears to be no record on the system but you will discuss it with the travel agent immediately. Contact the travel agent, explain the booking was not received and arrange relocation of the guest.
- Contact the travel agent to get confirmation of the booking for any bill-back purposes.
- NEVER blame the travel agent or accept liability. Just advise it is unusual for such an incident to occur and offer your apologies.

Guest screaming at you:

- Let them scream. They will soon run out of steam
- Stay calm and focused on dealing with the issues at hand.
- Do not scream back or raise your voice. Lower the tone of your voice to be more serious when speaking.
- Involve management if necessary
- As a last resort involves security if physical threats are made.

Emergency Measures:

Guest collapses:

- Keep calm!
- Ring the emergency services immediately
- Contact a manager or first aider
- Find out what medication the guest has taken/is taking, what they have eaten and any allergies or health conditions they may have – this is all information that the ambulance crew will need to know.
- Try to keep the guest conscious – do not move them unless you are a qualified first aider or the guest is in immediate danger.
- Close off access to the immediate area so that the incident is not viewed by other guests.

Armed Robbery

- This is very rare!
- Keep calm, quickly activate any silent alarm you may have installed
- Comply and carry out all instructions
- Do not try to overpower anyone who is armed – money can be replaced, you can't!

Guest has been robbed/incident of theft

- Immediately involve management
- Find out where the robbery took place and what was stolen
- Contact the police
- Immediately ensure that anyone in the area where the robbery took place is removed from the vicinity – evidence may be damaged or destroyed unknowingly

Emergency Measures:

Suspected food poisoning

- Immediately contact the kitchen and inform them so an incident report may be filed
- Involve senior hotel management
- Find out from the guest what they have eaten and where and get them to sign a confirmation of this
- Inform housekeeping so that any infection control policies can be implemented

Guest leaves without paying

- If you have contact details, contact them as soon as you become aware of the walk-out (for most guests it is a genuine mistake)
- If the guest has left their car with the valet or the keys are with reception, ensure that the relevant people are aware to refer the guest to reception to make payment prior to providing access to their vehicle.
- If the guest booked through a travel agent, contact the agent and ask them to contact the guest to arrange payment. If necessary, senior management may decide to invoice the travel agent for the unpaid amount.

A guest injures themselves

- Fill out the relevant accident report documentation
- Involve management
- Arrange medical assistance if necessary

Emergency Measures:

A bedroom goes out of order

- Arrange a repair as quickly as possible
- Put the room out of order in your property management/reservations system
- Move any guests in that room to an alternative room as quickly as possible

A guest damages their room

- Raise the appropriate charge and inform the guest of the reason for the charge
- If necessary refer to management to resolve and explain the nature of the charge

A guest smokes in their room

- In most hotels it is against the law to smoke in a room that is not designated as a smoking room (particularly within the UK).
- Guests should firstly be advised in writing via a letter in their room that continuing to smoke within the non-smoking room is forbidden or illegal and will result in a deep cleaning charge being added to their bill.
- Offer to move the guest to a smoking room (if you have them available) and advise on where the designated smoking areas are within the hotel.
- If the guest fails to comply, levy a deep cleaning charge and leave the room out of order for at least one day after they have departed to allow for the smell to dissipate.

Glossary

Adapted Room.
Sometimes referred to as 'disabled access room'. A room that has been modified for use by a wheelchair user; usually with lower light switches, emergency cords and assistance rails in the bathroom.

Allocation
The process of assigning rooms to guests. Also can mean the procedure of having a set amount of rooms reserved for a specific travel agent or price (e.g. there are 7 rooms allocated to them for that night)

Allocation Crossover
This is where a room type shows as available but no physical rooms can be allocated. This happens because a room is available on general availability but is not physically available in your inventory. This only tends to occur with stays of 2 nights or more.

Arrival
A guest who is due to check-in to the hotel.

Balancing Rooms
This is the procedure of changing reservation room types (e.g. from a standard double to a premium double) to avoid becoming overbooked on a specific room type. E.g. if you are overbooked by 2 doubles and have 3 premium doubles left to sell, your availability overall is one room but someone could still theoretically sell the 3 premium doubles, leaving you 2 rooms overbooked. Balancing by changing the room types (in this case changing 2 doubles to premium doubles) prevents this from occurring. This is extremely

Glossary

important when your system links to an online booking system such as Galileo or Worldspan (commonly used by travel agents)

Check-in
The process of registering a guest in to the hotel and providing them with a bedroom.

Check-in
The process of finalising a guest's stay and registering their vacating of their bedroom

Close-out
The process of stopping sales through one or many sources, such as websites and travel agents

Completion
The process of completing a pre-authorisation using the same authorisation code, thereby completing the sale and releasing any un-used amount to the card (e.g. the pre-authorization is for £20 and the completion is for £15 – the remaining £5 would then be released back to the card holders balance for them to access)

Cookie-Cutter
Where everything is the same and standard templates are used for everything – the same as making a batch of cookies using exactly the same cutter for each cookie, resulting in each cookie being the same!

Day Delegate
A guest who is attending an in-house conference or event and is using the hotel for only the day, they are not staying over at the hotel (a 24-Hour

Glossary

delegate is someone who is staying over at the hotel for one night or more whilst attending the conference)

Departure
A guest who is due to leave the hotel

ETA
Estimated time of arrival for the guest. Useful if you are expecting a VIP.

Folio
The guest's bill. Sometimes referred to as an invoice.

Last-Let
The worst rooms in the hotel, only used when absolutely necessary. Referred to as last let as they are used as a last resort for guests to stay in the hotel

Lock-out
When a guest has been locked out of their room

No Show
A guest with a reservation who did not check in to the hotel

Out booking
The process of moving a guest's reservation to an alternative hotel (usually due to availability)

Out of Order
The process of blocking a room from sale due to it being in an un-sellable condition (e.g. ceiling collapse, repairs or refurbishment). Putting a room out of order will stop that room from being sold until the room is put back in order.

Out of Service

The process of blocking a room from initial sale due to it being in a saleable, but less than perfect condition (e.g. recently painted, broken light bulb). Putting a room out of service will not stop the room from being sold, however it will restrict the room from being allocated unless specifically required (makes the room a 'last-let')

Overbooking

The process of having sold more rooms than you have in physical inventory in the hotel. Results in a negative availability figure.

Pre-Authorisation

The process of placing an authorisation on to a guests credit card to gain approval from the guest's bank or credit card company that the guest has sufficient funds to pay the amount due. This is followed by a completion upon checkout. The pre-authorisation will only 'freeze' the amount entered upon check-in. It does not debit the funds from the card but prevents the guest from accessing the amount of money held by the pre-authorisation. This allows the completion to occur without being declined due to lack of funds. The pre-authorisation will normally release after around 3-5 working days if the transaction is not completed.

Routing

The process of automatically setting the system to transfer one or more set charges to another room or account on your reservation system. Mainly used with larger, more advanced booking systems.

Glossary

Thank you for visiting! Have a nice day!

If you enjoyed this book, please review it as such and tell your friends!

If you have any questions please feel free to find me on twitter
@MShiells_Jones

Printed in Great Britain
by Amazon